WHEN SPIRITS SPEAK

*A down-to-earth,
straightforward system
for mastering mediumship*

MELISSA PHARR

When Spirits Speak
Copyright © 2025 Melissa Pharr

Paperback ISBN: 979-8-9922572-9-8

Praise for
When Spirits Speak

"If you have the gift of mediumship and want to develop your talent and make your greatest impact on the world, drop everything and read this book. Melissa Pharr is the most brilliant and comprehensive guide for how to develop as a medium!"

Sara Connell, bestselling author and founder of Thought Leader Academy

"This remarkable book offers an amazing step-by-step guide to mediumship for everyone. It is an extraordinary doorway to a path of personal growth and connection to Spirit, open to anyone ready to put forth the necessary commitment."

Rick Ansoff, Professor, National University and Medium

"Mel will draw you in on her wild, sometimes humorous, sometimes painful journey from business consultant to successful medium. The teachings she shares contain deep wisdom that will enrich the life of anyone, not just those looking to become a medium."

Amy F. Pelloquin, M.D.

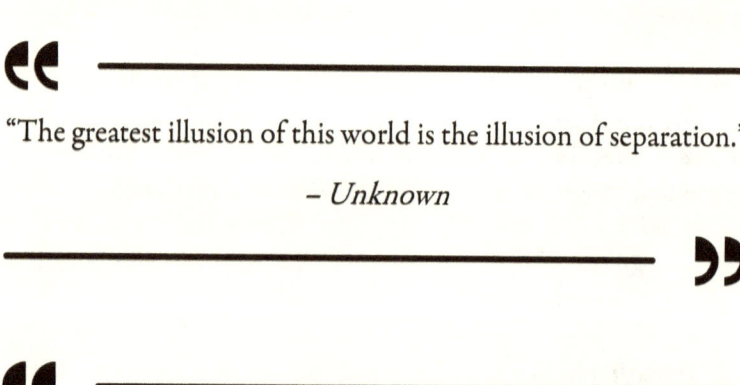

"The greatest illusion of this world is the illusion of separation."

– Unknown

"You do not need to work to become spiritual.
You are spiritual; you need only to remember that fact.
Spirit is within you. God is within you."

– Julia Cameron

For my daughters. May you quickly realize the power
of being profoundly connected to your own self,
to Spirit, and to all things.

Table of Contents

Introduction

I was tumbling into the deepest sleep you'd have ever thought possible during every 30-second break. As my body squeezed and tightened, I'd just barely awaken—arms, neck, and head hanging limply over the edges of the tub. There was no comfort. No respite, except for the warmth of the water that covered my massive belly and half of my bowling-ball tits that rose up out of the wet warmth. Rob was crouched down next to the tub with his fingers gently on my forehead.

"I don't think I can do this anymore," I croaked.

Concern and love emanated from his kind eyes—his feature I'd always loved best and noticed from the first day we'd met. I hadn't heard any movement near the end of the bathtub, but one of our midwives was crouched down and looking sympathetic. "Mel, we've all been discussing your options, and we think it's the safest decision to transfer you to the hospital. You haven't dilated past six centimeters for the past 34 hours. I'm sorry. I know you wanted to have the baby here."

"Awesome," I slurred sincerely. My midwife looked surprised as I continued, "It's ok. I just want this over with. I'm following the path of this birth." She smiled gently, looking sad but relieved.

Paramedics entered shortly after with a gurney that I suppose they thought I'd be lying down on to be rolled like a beached whale out of the birthing center. The thought of gravity pulling down on my belly and body would be nothing less than extreme torture at this point. I overheard my midwife, Aubrey, speaking to one of them. "I don't think she'll want the fentanyl…"

I mustered every ounce of energy as I haggardly croaked with desperation, "Give me the fucking fentanyl. And PS, I'm not lying down on that gurney. I'll walk." I've never been someone who liked to mince words.

Five hours later at the hospital—39 hours of labor total, including pitocin and every physical exercise known to birthing people to encourage the baby along—I knew this baby was still convinced that coming earthside via the vagina was a no-go. As my care team came together to suggest that a cesarean was best, they were pleasantly surprised by my joy at being one step closer to finally meeting my daughter after nearly 42 weeks of pregnancy.

Rob sat closely behind me in a scrub cap and surgical mask, his soft and gentle eyes looking into mine.

"I'm so cold. I can't stop shaking," I shivered, "Is this normal?" I asked the anesthesiologist.

"Yes, but I know it's uncomfortable," he offered sympathetically.

"How soon will I get my baby?"

"In about 15 seconds, ma'am." He smiled excitedly. "As long as everything looks good, we'll put her on your chest right away, as you requested."

My heart leapt, and the pounding in my chest went full blast. I didn't know how many midwives and doctors were in the room along with the surgeon, but I'll never forget the perfect lineup of exclamations I heard shortly after the tugging sensations on the lower half of my body subsided.

"She's *so* pink!"

"She's *huge*!"

"She's beautiful!"

"Look at those *cheeks*! No wonder she wouldn't come out!"

My beautiful baby Bea punctuated their celebrations with a cry that I'll remember forever. My whole body shook from the frosty feeling of cold and the tears that poured down my cheeks. I knew that she had *finally* arrived whole and healthy. During a cesarean, your upper body is tilted downward slightly. This made it difficult to see much when a pair of arms held out the massive, nearly 10-pound bundle toward me and set her gently upon my chest.

Her warm body heated mine. I couldn't see her face clearly. Instead, I inhaled her baby scent and sobbed while I fingered her tiny wrinkly hands. Rob smiled and helped me hold her tightly against myself as I continued to shiver from the anesthesia.

Any human who has witnessed new life coming into this world knows the profound and miraculous feeling that overwhelms and overcomes us in so many different expressions.

Little did I know that in a relatively short period of time, I'd be forever changed once again. This time, not by life entering this world, but instead by discovering the life that exists after physical death, when spirits speak.

• • •

In this book, you can expect to hear the whole unfiltered truth about how my awareness of my mediumistic skills came about and just how skeptical I was during that part of my journey. I'll share my passionate stance on why mediumship matters so very much as a practice, and most of all, I can't wait to share with you, in my organized, structured, and step-by-step style, a powerful and strategic system for developing your own mediumship skills. If I do say so myself, this intangible and elusive work could use a teacher, or many, with an analytical mind and who is willing to go deep with the nitty-gritty details of how spirit communication works. The best news is, you've found her.

I wouldn't be the only person to tell you that I hold nothing back. Although it is a self-proclamation at this moment, my students will tell you that I share, in as much detail as possible, every aspect of my experience and the juicy behind-the-scenes details—in order to help more spiritual practitioners do their best work and feel joy and confidence while they're at it. If you've been looking for more than vague descriptions of mediumship how-tos and you're ready to learn in a way that truly takes you to the next level, you've arrived at the right place.

Perhaps the most unique thing about this book that I know you haven't seen before, because it's my own original creation, is my Mediumship Development Framework that features what I call the five Cs. These five Cs are what I've found to be the most crucial aspects of mediumship development. They are: Becoming a Clear Channel, Spirit Communication and the Clairs, Confidence, Community, and developing a Command of your Craft.

I'll be taking you through each of the Cs step-by-step and providing explanations that make this ethereal work easier to understand. There are exercises galore to help you practically apply what you learn and advance your skills more effectively and efficiently.

If there's one powerful lesson that mediumship has taught me, it is to trust our path as spiritual beings inside of these human bodies. This applies to the unfolding of our spiritual gifts and to our life experience. I never expected to become a spiritual medium. If you'd have asked me about my professional future just two years before writing this book, I would have laughed if you'd have told me this would be it.

I wrote this book not solely because I felt like it'd be nice to put my knowledge into something easily accessible that could reach and help more people. I wrote this book because it was waiting to write itself and couldn't be helped. It poured out of me once I found myself in this space, and now, after years of wondering where I was needed next, I've discovered my place.

I practice mediumship for many reasons, but the most important is the power it holds to heal divides and remind us that we are all profoundly connected with each other and all living things here and beyond. It's a catalyst to dissolving barriers that leave us separate and stop us from moving forward to create a better world.

The evidence that comes through during a reading and proves that our consciousness survives the death of the body is wild. Even more spectacular is the experience of seeing that no matter our differences, when someone sits down in front of you as a medium, you hear many of the same basic desires, needs, fears, hopes, and dreams unearthed through readings. It's undeniable how much we all have in common. To be enveloped by the overwhelming feeling of love and interconnectedness that comes from this work is to realize how our perspectives of ourselves and others change when our hearts are opened, how our "us vs. them" mentality is shed.

It is my hope that you know deeply within yourself that if you've been pulled, even a little, in this direction of mediumship and spiritual development, it is meant for you. Not only that, but it has so very much to offer. It very well may save your life, and at the very least, it will change your life—and for the better.

Whether you have aspirations to strengthen your spiritual senses for your own benefit, you long to work professionally, or anything in between, my wish for you is to be empowered to connect with these innate gifts of yours and to use them in your own unique and remarkable way, for good.

Before we continue, it's essential that I share with you the definitions of a few terms I'll be using throughout this book. In my time talking to dead people and through my studies with mentors that I respect and trust, I've come to believe that we are all connected as one through consciousness. This all-one consciousness that continues after the death of the physical body is what I call the Spirit World and will reference throughout this book as Spirit with a capital S. Think of this all-one consciousness as the mothership of all of our individual spirits that come together as one.

When I am speaking about an individual spirit, or a group of individual spirits that are communicating with me as a medium, I will use the word spirit, or spirits, with a lower case s. It's important to note that different people have different belief systems. Some speak or pray to Spirit, while others may reference this same all one consciousness as God, Source, or another term. Others believe in both God and Spirit but view them separately.

There are times when I will ask my students to make a connection with their higher self. I define the higher self as the purely spiritual aspect of our individual selves. I will also reference spirit guides, those spiritual beings that help us along our life path, and angels as well. Angels are spiritual entities that exist at a higher vibrational frequency, and many mediums believe they have never walked the earth.

If I'm honest with you, I don't consider myself the resident expert on these different spiritual entities. It seems silly to me to convey absolute confidence in something that is so intangible to most human beings, that I don't remember encountering after a previous death, and, as of yet, that I haven't heard much about through my conversations with spirits that I've communicated with.

Lastly, if I speak about "transitioning" or "passing," this means dying. If I mention the "other side," I'm talking about where we go after we die to join the mothership of all one consciousness, the Spirit World. When I use the term "sitter," I'm not talking about childcare. I'm referring to the person who sits with a medium to receive a reading. Finally, a "spiritual impression" is a single thought that a spirit sends to a medium via any of the clair senses in order to communicate.

Want to start strengthening your clair senses now as you read this book? Use this QR code below to learn three easy exercises to strengthen your clairs and speak to Spirit!

01
How I Discovered
I'm a Medium

In 2019, I was on a Q&A call for my group program for entrepreneurs. I was coaching a client who was explaining to me the service she was looking to offer.

"So my clients come into a six week program I've designed where we get in touch with their true self. My question is, I'm wondering if you think six weeks is long enough of a program?"

I was cringing inside as I listened to her question.

"Okay, I'm going to need a little more information about what it is you're offering, Jenny. What are they struggling with when they come to you? What's the result they get from working with you? What modalities do you use with your clients to help them go from where they are to where they want to be?"

Jenny was silent for a few moments. "Well, they feel stuck when they come to me, and after we work together, they feel more confident, and they are able to manifest what they want in life, I guess... I'm guided by my intuition when I work with clients, so it's kind of different for all of them and hard to be specific."

This was going to be a painful conversation. More than 40% of my clients were running businesses that were considered to be in the intuitive and spiritual industries, and I often found that these clients struggled to craft specific and compelling language around their offers. For me, it was like pulling teeth, and it had me feeling skeptical about this kind of airy-fairy work that seemed to entail crystals, tarot cards, and all kinds of spiritual stuff that I wasn't convinced made much of a difference. In my world, if I wanted to make something happen, I just did it.

It wasn't that I was a cold-hearted bitch lacking any empathy at all or that I hadn't been on the struggle bus myself as an entrepreneur. Rob had seen me go from a sinking entrepreneur when we met in 2011 to a seven-figure business owner. He'd believed in me back in 2014 when I was $42,000 in debt and five years into an entrepreneurial journey that didn't seem to be going anywhere. Maybe it was because, at that point, he truly saw in me what I'd only caught glimmers of in hopeful and fleeting moments.

Maybe his love and belief backing me is what finally did it. That same year, in 2014, I had paid off 100% of my debt and created my first $250,000-revenue year. I spent the next seven years teaching women entrepreneurs to create six-figure, multi-six-figure, and seven-figure businesses as an online marketing strategist. Rob watched me sell hundreds of courses online, build a marketing program for women that more than 500 clients graduated from, host live three-day events in New York City with attendees from all over the world, and more. He supported my every dream with unshakeable belief and unconditional love.

As time went on though, I was growing tired of answering the same questions and helping my clients create language that got to the heart of what was so amazing and unique about their work. Truly, every client I worked with had something incredible to offer, and I genuinely believed in each of them. I even considered myself somewhat spiritual, but couldn't these people be a little more specific and structured and a little less unicorns and rainbows? *If I were some kind of spiritual practitioner*, I told myself, *I could figure it out ASAP. Of course*, I chuckled as I sprawled in my desk chair, legs up by my keyboard, *it would be laughable to imagine myself in an industry like that.*

That year, 2019, about a year before I became pregnant with my daughter, it had become clear that it was time to make a change. It took almost two years, but by the time Bea arrived in 2021, I had retired my online marketing business. After years of hard work and long hours, I was ready for a break. Rob and I had discussed my plan. Our plan. I felt so certain, as I usually do, when I told him as confidently as ever, "I'll know what I'm doing next by the time she's two years old. Right now, I just want to take this time off from working to be a Mom. I want to enjoy this break until I discover what's next."

20 Months Later

I truly had a strong inner knowing that by Bea's second birthday, I'd know exactly what my next steps would be as a financially contributing member of our small family of three. Maybe that was just something that I was telling myself, and I was no longer the clear and confident woman and business owner that I'd learned to see myself as.

Here we were, in October of 2022, just four months away from Bea's second birthday, and for the first time in my life, I had zero clarity or insight into a future career for myself. It was a foreign feeling not to have a plan and to be all-in. I'd had fleeting moments of excitement about ideas here or there, but I found that nothing I'd spent my time doing in the past held any interest for me. I couldn't will myself to get excited about anything for long, and I didn't recognize this version of myself who felt purposeless and unmotivated beyond my role as a new parent.

Every piece of my identity that I'd learned to take pride in was gone. During the pandemic, we left New York City for the summer to stay near my sister in Montana and never returned.

Instead, we bought our first car and drove to Colorado to fulfill a dream we'd been pursuing for three years. I knew I'd found my meant-to-be home, but New Yorker to Coloradan, non-parent to parent, athletic and fit to postpartum recovery, and, most of all, successful entrepreneur to stay-at-home parent with no clue what I had to offer any longer... I wasn't feeling like myself. I was a bit of a shitshow.

• • •

Rob had just started traveling to New York for work, and I had some quiet evenings to myself after putting Bea to bed. These were the nights when I turned to my enabling companion, Netflix. Why not get a workout in while finishing the final episode of a TV series I binged with my best friend and her wife during a long weekend visit I'd recently come home from.

I grabbed the only workout mat in our bedroom. Ugh, it was Rob's blue yoga mat that he refused to throw away. He'd told me he liked that it had extra cushion for his knees. Apparently I was the only one who minded that it was profusely shedding, leaving tiny bits of blue spongy fuzz everywhere in the house. I set my laptop on the bed and propped it up, slightly lopsided, on a large squashy pillow. As the intro played, I gathered my weights and workout bands. I felt purposeless without a business to run, but I still managed to think of lists of to-dos each day to drown the voice inside that kept reminding me I no longer had anything to offer professionally.

The episode was called "*Are You An Intuit?*" It featured a famous medium named Laura Lynn Jackson, whom I'd never heard of before. I wasn't sure what "mediums" even did. I'd had a client who was a medium and gave me some sort of session once. Interestingly, she was spot on about the birth of my daughter, but I couldn't remember anything else about the experience.

Laura Lynn Jackson was teaching a class and then giving "readings" to people where she apparently communicated wildly accurate details of the people's loved ones who'd died. I'd watched more than half of the episode and worked up a bit of a sweat too.

At this point, Laura was sitting in a chair across from a client, rattling off details that were supposedly coming through from a deceased person. I was holding weights in each hand and doing side lunges, huffing and puffing through the set. The person she was sitting with looked confused and kept saying "No, none of this makes sense." Suddenly a member of the camera crew burst into tears and validated every word Laura Lynn Jackson had said.

As the episode went on to explain that spirits associated with anyone in the room can visit, I started to get a strange, sudden, and strong feeling of déjà vu. In my own mind, or my imagination, I supposed, I was sitting in the chair, as if I *was* Laura Lynn Jackson. It was as if I was *giving* the reading that I was watching her deliver. I felt aching in my core and lower body only to realize that I'd been paused in a side lunge and zoning out into space. I continued to focus intently on what I was seeing as I straightened and simultaneously dropped the weights to the floor. As I watched Laura Lynn read, a feeling of unexpected familiarity came over me emotionally—and even physically. I experienced what I can only describe as a deep sense of well-being and overwhelming love, while any awareness of my physical body was gone. A thought popped into my head that was more of a *knowing*.

"I *know* how to do that. I've *known* how to do that for a long, long time. I *can* do that, right now, today."

Those thoughts are what finally snapped me out of it. *What just happened? Why did watching this medium make me imagine that I had any of these abilities?* For what seemed like minutes, I was held in a daze and unable to muster any other thoughts at all. Once I did, the episode was nearly over. I glanced at my weights to recall whether or not I'd finished my final set.

I slowly walked to my bed and sat down. I needed a moment to figure this out. I supposed that every human who sees this kind of thing questions whether it's really possible, and if it is, wonders if it's possible for them. This was different, though. I knew what it felt like to ponder possibilities. This experience was out of the body as if I'd been temporarily transported back in time to what seemed like a previous life experience.

As I sat on my bed, stunned, an image of myself confidently relaying information to someone, from a person who had died, floated into my mind. I couldn't see myself in the image. I was in a dark room. I could tell that I had a dress on and brown shoes because I was looking through my own eyes at a woman sitting in front of me who seemed emotional. These moments were only in my mind, like a daydream, and yet as they happened, it was as if I had very little awareness of anything else.

I shook my head as if to wipe my mind clean of the image I was seeing. I'm not a medium who gets the chills often, though many mediums do, but I watched as the hair raised on my forearms and goosebumps followed. I stared at my arms, feeling confused. Was this real? Could I really talk to dead people? During this bizarre experience, I felt much more than convinced. I knew that I could.

It was only moments later that both excitement and anxiety washed over me. As instantly as those feelings had come, they immediately vanished. I began to reason with myself. *You're tired, Mel. You're single parenting this week with an almost two-year-old. Things always seem stranger at night, but you'll come to your senses in the morning.* As I talked myself through these more logical thoughts, embarrassment and shame surfaced. Who was I? A narcissistic asshole who liked to watch professionals—who had put countless hours into their craft—perform their incredible work and then casually act as if I was God's gift?

After my experience in the coaching world, I could only imagine that in an unregulated spiritual industry, countless humans acted as proclaimed experts after a ten-minute-or-less training. Maybe feeling purposeless was taking more of a toll than I'd realized. Perhaps I was trying to prove something to Rob or myself about still being a useful and contributing member of our family—and society. I went through the motions of getting ready for bed in a bit of daze and after thirty minutes of racing thoughts coursing through my brain subsided, I finally fell asleep.

• • •

A week passed, and my intrigue grew into ceaseless curiosity about this new thing called mediumship. Perhaps I should just forget about that strange experience and get myself back into meditation. I'd grown to love meditation over the past years, but I'd lapsed on the practice since my daughter arrived. I felt pulled toward meditation now, and in all honesty, I hoped that it might stifle my interest in this strange and bizarre thing I'd discovered.

As I sat down to take my attention to my breath, I relaxed into the state that I'd missed so much. I let my mind release and my thoughts go blank. I'd come to crave this habit while practicing more regularly, and I was quickly reminded of why. As I let go of the present moment, I began to experience the strangest sensation. In each of my hands, I felt another hand holding mine. I instantly felt as if I *knew* that these were the hands of each of my deceased grandmothers. I wasn't afraid, but I threw my eyes open to see if Grandma Ann and Grandma Shirley were actually there. The sensation of their touch diminished only slightly as I looked around the room, double checking that I was alone. I felt silly, but even stronger was the pull to continue and see where this led. I closed my eyes again and focused on the feeling of their hands in mine. As I did, my heart swelled, and I felt overcome with the strongest feeling of unconditional love from both of my grandmothers. It was warm all around my body, and I somehow sensed that I was being energetically surrounded in their embrace.

I was feeling more emotionally vulnerable with every moment, as if long-held feelings of anger, resentment, and frustration were on the brink of bubbling up and spilling out everywhere before they melted away. What if Bea or Rob burst into the room? How would I explain this moment? My worries quickly subsided as a sense of safety came over me. I was receiving a new idea in my mind and "heard" what seemed to be thoughts pouring into my head from my paternal grandmother. "I forgive you, although I know you haven't asked for forgiveness. I understand why you didn't want to speak to me. I realize now how difficult it was to be around me."

Emotions of shame and guilt that I must have pushed down far enough to escape my awareness rose to the surface. I was overcome with grief, relief, and love all at once. My paternal grandmother passed away in October of 2020, and I had barely spoken to her for nine years before she died, in person or on the phone. It wasn't a consciously deliberate choice, but she wasn't a happy person, and she'd lived a hard life. The last few times we'd spoken, I would ask her how she was. She'd usually say, "Just waiting to die," and she meant it. I found it painful to interact with her, and it kept me away.

I'm not sure how long the experience lasted, but I know I sobbed and shook for at least three or four minutes while I continued to feel the presence of both grandmothers. It was a therapeutic release. A letting go of something I hadn't even realized wasn't dealt with. I sat in silence as their presence suddenly drifted away and continued to focus on my breath. It seemed like the natural thing to do, and it was what I needed at that moment.

When I finally opened my eyes, my shoulders were hanging limply by my side, and I felt peaceful—albeit a bit strange—emotional, and exhausted. *Something* had clearly happened, and it had affected more than just my emotions. Despite the feeling of peace, my mind was confused by the experience, and my body was tired.

• • •

It was a week before I shared my experience with Rob. He's my go-to person and best friend, and this is the one time in our lives together that I can recall intentionally keeping something from him for an entire week.

What if I *was* losing my mind? Could it be early-onset dementia? I was only 38, but was that *possible?* Had these identity shifts shaken me to the core to the point that I desperately needed to lie and make up stories to reclaim my feeling of worth and to receive attention? I felt more sane than ever, but perhaps humans often do when they start to lose it?

While I was distressed by these strange experiences, I felt excitement and anticipation brewing—as if something was coming that would change me. I felt too embarrassed to share the latter with anyone, but I had a plan that consisted of a single next step to figure out what was happening to me.

The next time Rob traveled to New York, I planned a night of my own to sit in silence and see what oddities might unfold. In addition to Rob, I had confided in a dear friend. Her father had passed away some years ago, but we hadn't spoken about him much. As I sat in silence on the couch, I suddenly became aware of the energetic presence of someone standing next to me, the same way you might get the impression of a person loitering behind you. I couldn't see anyone, but it only took a moment to sense it, like a fuzzy-static-electricity type of feeling, and within seconds, it became stronger. I asked myself, *Am I sensing a man standing beside me?* I quickly confirmed to myself, *Yes, I am.*

I had that same *knowing* that it was my friend's father that I'd had with my grandmothers. Thoughts of him seemed to drift into my mind, as if I could hear inside my head what he wanted to say.

"I wasn't strong enough to continue on in this life. Tell her I'll be with her when her son is born."

This time, along with *hearing* him, I also sensed the type of person he had been when he was alive—a sensitive man. Kind. And broken-hearted and suffering during much of his time on earth.

What was I supposed to do with this information, this experience? I'd been watching YouTube videos and Netflix documentaries. I'd started reading books, too, anything I could get my hands on that would save me from facing the truth about my potentially shattering sanity. I'd learned that it wasn't ethical to share information with people about their passed loved ones without their consent and thorough understanding of the mediumship process. They could be in any state of emotional instability or grief. They could be in a great place in life, and hearing from their passed loved ones could threaten that if it wasn't the right time and place.

Although I saw my friend every week, I kept my visit with her father to myself. Who was I to emotionally manipulate a pregnant woman who was my friend and whom I loved dearly? I wouldn't be that person. It wasn't until I entered her house near the end of her pregnancy and she announced that perhaps her water had broken that I felt I was getting pelted with signs to relay the message. When she asked me directly to share with her my mediumship news, I burst into tears and then asked permission to share the experience. She validated that how I'd sensed her dad was how he had been, and forty-eight hours later, her beautiful son was born.

At this point, things started to seem like perhaps there was a sliver of validity to them. I continued to have experiences that seemed uncanny and even hired two different mediums. One referenced the message I'd received from my paternal grandmother, and the other brought through "the father of my close friend who had a new baby boy" and said the message from him was for my own validation as a medium. With every experience, I was more floored than before.

My mother-in-law once said to me, "You don't do anything halfway, do you, Mel?" She was right, more or less, and I moved forward with some deciding steps.

First, I made the decision to put these potential skills to the test with a real person. I would reach out to someone and ask if they'd allow me to try out giving a reading as a medium. I was at a mama meetup with my daughter when I heard in my mind, as clear as day,

"Ask Abby." You'd think I would've felt embarrassed or even nervous about approaching someone, but I didn't. This knowing feeling within myself was peculiar, and it continued to strengthen with every experience I was having. Somehow I knew she would be perfect. I approached this woman who I barely knew and filled her in on what might potentially be my newfound gifts. I oddly didn't feel too strange, but I distinctly remember consciously acting as calm and "normal" as possible in case I was off my nut and didn't know it. I'd met her a handful of times, and she was always so very open and friendly. As soon as I began sharing my story, a grin spread over her face. When I got to the point of asking if she was up for being my guinea pig, she said excitedly without a beat, "I *love* stuff like this. My mom has been to mediums before. I'd *love* to!"

A week later, we sat in my family room. I made sure to be honest and transparent about my absolute lack of experience but my dire need to see what might happen. She was clear on the situation and fully ready. I wanted to manage her expectations, so I told her to be prepared for ten minutes of absolute silence and nothing but a whole lot of diddly-dick happening.

I began by quieting my mind as I would if I were sitting in meditation. At first, there was nothing, just silence and the odd sound of a settling house. Then, within moments, I noticed the feeling of fuzzy energy on my right side. The thing that I'll never forget was how it blew my mind just how *subtle* the tiny inklings of communication from a spirit actually are. So subtle indeed that if the feeling of spirit communication has never been explained to you, you'd easily miss it altogether or feel certain that it was merely your imagination. The first thing I understood about the energy that I was sensing was that it was feminine. This spirit had been a woman when she was living. As I leaned into these sensations, the fuzzy energy split in two, and although I wasn't quite sure, I decided to trust my interpretation that was leading me to believe there were two spirits present. Within moments, I sensed and *knew* that her grandmother and aunt, both on her mother's side, were present. I can't say how I knew, except that in my mind's eye, I caught quick glimpses of their stature and some facial features, however obscurely they were coming across. I also got the feeling of an aunt-like figure and a grandmother-like figure, the same way that you would if you met someone and they came across in that way.

The moment I revealed their identities, Abby burst into tears and began nodding her head. Somewhere in the mix, I got up to grab a box of tissues, which luckily was nearby. As I shared what was coming to me, the two spirits gave me more information. I knew details of their passing and the timing, their character and personality, and their closest living family members.

At one point when I felt connected to her grandmother, I saw a short video reel type of image in my mind, but up and off to my right side. It was her grandmother's thumbs and pointer fingers holding a necklace that she was swinging back and forth. On the necklace was something round. I was in awe as I identified this round item as a small silver medal from a vocal competition I'd won in high school. I knew in that moment somehow that the object, of course, wasn't what was hanging from her grandmother's necklace, but that she was communicating to me that the object's roundness was significant. When I told Abby this, she gasped loudly as her hand went to her mouth.

"I have that necklace at my house right now. My grandmother's wedding ring is hanging from it!" I was in too much shock to remember a lot of details about my reaction to the necklace, but I'm pretty sure I was only a few seconds away from shitting myself. Even so, it just kept coming. I saw a knitted shawl of some kind next and described it to Abby. She told me it was hanging over a chair at her house and that she hadn't washed it because it smelled like her grandmother. I was shown memories of the end-of-life goodbye for her aunt who was lying in a hospital bed, unresponsive, with family members sharing their farewells. I told Abby that she had heard and understood those words, and tears continued to pour down her face.

As the reading went on, the information flowed, and I lost track of time, but I do recall how it ended. When the information slowed and the most important messages felt as if they had been delivered, I told Abby that I was ready to leave her with their love. We paused for a moment in utter silence. I remember one of us saying, "Holy shit!" and within an instant we both burst into hardcore ugly cries that were cathartic and filled with love, healing, and excitement. For Abby, perhaps it was something she had already believed in and had an understanding of, but for me, I was in awe of the apparent way that this world worked and the magic that surrounds us that I'd known almost nothing about.

I was in disbelief. How could I feel *who* they were and *how* they were so easily? Not only that, but I was able to relay messages from both of these spirits that were incredibly meaningful and significant not just to Abby, but to her mother, who texted me shortly after the reading to give her thanks. Abby sent a text as well, with pictures of the shawl and necklace that I had seen.

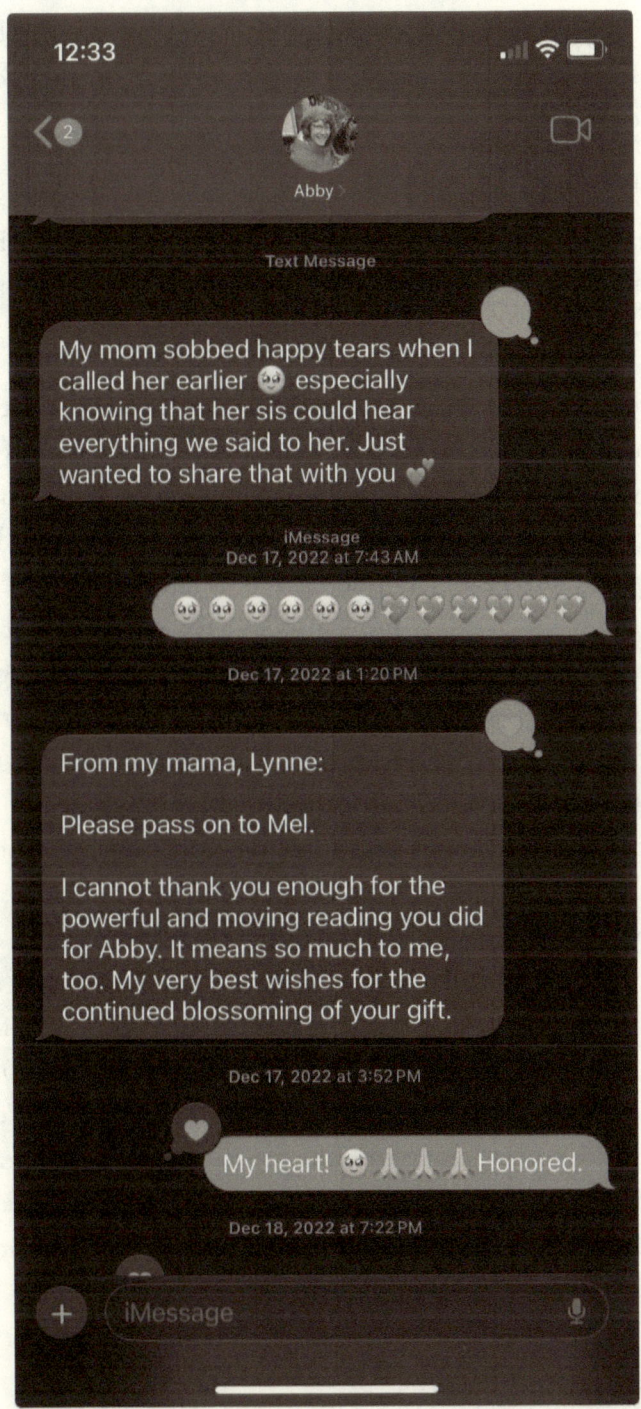

When Rob came down the steps from his office after Abby left, he must have seen the dazed and shocked look on my face as I struggled to process what had just happened.

"Are you ok?" he inquired.

I was silent for a beat and said, "You're not gonna fuckin' believe what just happened." I breathed as I shook my head incredulously.

• • •

My second deciding step was to give 100 free readings. What could teach me better than experience? I was lucky to have friends in my new town who seemed to know absolutely everyone. Before long, I'd give a reading, and multiple referrals would come in within days or sometimes hours. Not every reading flew by like that first one, but I was generally always able to bring through a recognizable spirit, often with some considerably jaw-dropping evidence, and a message that deeply resonated with my sitter. Before long, I was getting more than a dozen texts, emails, or calls a week. Rob asked me to start giving readings virtually over zoom instead of having people we didn't know come to the house, and I felt the same. Not everyone has positive feelings toward the practice of mediumship, and some of my newfound medium friends that I'd met in my first few virtual classes had told me their family members believed that speaking to spirits was evil and against their religious beliefs. I'd heard stories from a mentor who had been giving in-person readings for nearly 30 years. She had had some frightening experiences where she'd felt uncomfortable being alone with the people she was giving readings to. Some had been sexual predators, some were journalists looking to paint her as a fraud, and some were offended enough by the practice that they meant harm via verbal abuse.

My third deciding step came when I asserted that if I was going to do this, I wanted to do the absolute best I could. Mediumship was undoubtedly a huge responsibility, and I didn't take it, or the ongoing education it required, lightly. I sat down with Rob and told him I had picked out a weeklong residential class at Arthur Findlay College in Essex in the UK. This was apparently one of the most well-known and highly regarded places to study. The class began in three weeks. Rob smiled, "I guess we'll have to arrange some extra childcare then. Maybe your parents would be willing to drop Bea off at preschool in the mornings?"

• • •

My time at Arthur Findlay College (AFC) was a dream. Not only did I meet wonderful people who were surprisingly normal and as excited, passionate, and weirded out as I was, but the teachers were kind, encouraging, and enjoyable to learn from. Walking down a hallway at AFC was like visiting an old stately home. I saw black and white photos of mediums from earlier generations, a large staircase draped in crimson red carpet, and old furniture that creaked when I sat down.

I definitely sensed that spirits were all around me, but I didn't feel spooked. It was like being at the real-life Hogwarts in some ways. Most importantly, I got what I came for: significant validation that what I was experiencing was in fact, real. There are only so many times you can sit down with someone and know specific and significant details about their life and their passed loved ones' lives before you feel you can't deny that communication with those who have left this earth is possible. There are ample opportunities while you study there to get the proof you may desperately need that you're not batshit crazy, with the twelve-hour-long days chock-full of practice sessions, teachings, talks, and demonstrations of all kinds.

When I arrived back home in Colorado, I was hooked. Finally, I had discovered what was next for me and something that would enable me to make a contribution that *truly* mattered and might change people's lives for the better.

I got straight to work continuing to move through my 100 free readings. I documented in a journal—in detail—every reading up to number seventy-two. As I reviewed my readings, I got even more out of them, writing down my learnings while keeping an additional journal where I notated symbols I used during readings. As my confidence grew, I quickly set up an Instagram account and dug out an old YouTube course I'd bought four years prior and never started. Clearly it was meant for this business and not my previous one. Ideas and content seemed to pour out of me. I recorded every reading and collected testimonials as I went, along with permission from those who consented for me to use my readings on YouTube and show what a mediumistic experience with me was like. I wrote the content for my website in three hours from a coffee shop and reached out to a past team member to see if she could get me up and running with a website in the following weeks.

It was nearly seven months total between that first practice reading that blew my mind in December of 2022 and my first professional reading that came after my thirty-ninth birthday in June of 2023. When I turn around and look back at that time, I can hardly believe how quickly things changed. It felt like my every move was supported by a powerful undercurrent that took on most of the hard work. Don't get me wrong, I logged the hours and put in the time. I have recordings of readings coming out of my ears and YouTube videos ready for publishing that stretched forward for an entire year. Still, I can't ignore how easily it all unfolded or how I felt like I was sitting on a magic carpet and being delivered to my next chapter with the support of something powerful behind me.

Not to say that coming out about my mediumistic skills was a walk in the park. I had my share of emails from my previous online audience informing me that I was doing the devil's work, plus some bumpy conversations in my family and friend group that took a while to work through. While my mom in particular was extremely supportive, we had a funny conversation one night during a routine game of Catan after my parents had come for dinner. She had fully supported my decisions to dive in head-first and believed in me. My parents often watched new YouTube videos I'd publish of my readings, and I could tell the first few times she watched that it spooked her a bit, "Can I ask you a question?"

"Sure," I wasn't sure where this was going, but I could already sense it wasn't personal, just pure curiosity coming from a brain that'd been slightly befuddled by my still-recent medium news.

"Well, what would you think if I told you that *I* was starting to hear spirits and communicate with them?" She leaned in across the table studying me.

"Easy. I'd most definitely worry that you were experiencing the early stages of dementia."

"What? I mean, yes, yes! Me too!" She exclaimed with relief at my understanding of her point.

"I totally get it, Mom. It's not that you don't trust me or believe me. It's just that it's really hard to wrap your mind around, isn't it?"

"It really is, Melissa." I could tell she was relieved in some way to feel safe sharing the truth of where her head was at with all of this.

"I know. I agree. I feel like that some days myself." We moved onto our board game, and that was that.

In a beautiful way, mediumship has allowed me to feel an even deeper connection with my Mom, who is a steadfast Catholic with a deep commitment to her faith. Christianity, and religion in general, is not something I feel called to, but I've found that we share many common values and both have our own version of faith that we can find common ground with. Without a doubt, my practice of speaking to Spirit has only brought us closer. For this, my gratitude is abounding. After all, never, in a single reading, has a spirit come to discuss the amount of money they had, the car they drove, how big their flat screen TV was, what their house cost, or anything that has much to do with material objects, with the exception of keepsakes that have been left behind and hold great value to those still living, as a means of evidence. Instead, the messages that come through are messages about people, relationships, love, thanks, remorse, apologies, acknowledgements, encouragement, and validations. They are about the kinds of things that hold the greatest opportunities to remind us of the nearly inconceivable and miraculously elaborate connection between all living things. From my time so far speaking with Spirit, it seems there is an all-encompassing oneness that governs this planet and universe that we live in. Even more, in my experience, I've found that when we touch upon that oneness and share it with others, our hard exteriors soften. That oneness is what unifies us and changes our hearts and minds.

Since beginning my work as a medium professionally, I've offered mediumistic readings, spiritual assessments for those looking to develop their intuitive or mediumistic gifts, mediumship development circles, courses, workshops, a deck, and this book. I've been blown away by the response as my offers sell out completely each and every time they are presented. It goes to show that there is a hunger for this work and for deeper discovery about what exists that we can't hold in our hands or see with our eyes. People want answers to their questions about why we're here and what happens when we die. They are looking for hope, connection, and an answer to the division that characterizes our countries and the world. I do believe that mediumship holds many of the most powerful answers.

02
Why Mediumship Matters

There is no doubt that we are living in a time of great division, and not just within a particular country, but globally. No matter when you read this book, humankind will always be making its way through periods of significant division and periods of greater peace. This usually comes back to economic uncertainty, war, political division, etc.

No matter our grievances, it seems that division itself is as dangerous as any one challenge that we face. Division is what causes fear and makes us forget all of the many things that we have in common. It stops us from solving our challenges. As we dig in our heels without effort toward empathy, understanding, and compromise, the distance widens, and we solidify our "us vs. them" mentalities that seem to keep us from progressing forward.

And yet, something much stronger than hope remains for us as the "innately spiritual beings" that Lisa Miller, a clinical psychologist at Teachers College, Columbia University, shares that we now know we are, based on 20 years of research and peer reviewed science. In times of division, even as we struggle to agree on much, we long for understanding, mercy, empathy, and connection. Think about how you gravitate toward those who offer you acceptance, comfort, and community in times of trial and isolation. Recall the excruciating feeling of frustration that overtakes us when we can't seem to wrap our minds around the differing views and beliefs of others. Beneath our finger pointing is a visceral craving for clarity and understanding.

Perhaps the fact that we are innately spiritual not only pulls us toward this need to comprehend our situation and experience togetherness but also accounts for the shift toward spirituality during divisive times. After all, the spiritual aspect of us that recognizes we are all one does not judge, condemn or exclude others based on their gender, age, (dis)ability, race, religion, lack of religion, sexual orientation, or political affiliation, among other things that we spend our time arguing about.

I know this from my many conversations with those on the other side who now, as spirit people, offer apologies for prioritizing their ego-based views of human identity over the sharing of unconditional love with those they encountered while they were living. Gravitating toward that spiritual aspect of ourselves is what leads us to a place of greater unity that we ultimately desire.

In 2023, seven out of ten Americans identified themselves as spiritual, whether they associated with an organized religion or not, according to a Pew Research study. While a trend toward spirituality during challenging times does not translate into a belief in the practice of spiritual or psychic mediumship, according to IBISWorld's 2024 "Psychic Services in the US" industry analysis presented by Michal Dalal,[1] *"A long-term shift in consumer perceptions has underpinned growth as mainstream consumers increasingly accept psychic services. Traditional skepticism about consulting psychics has waned, with more consumers embracing these services, especially in times of uncertainty."*

---

[1] https://www.ibisworld.com/united-states/market-research-reports/psychic-services-industry/

Yes, there is still plenty of skepticism surrounding mediumship and psychic work, but we certainly are no longer living in a time when most mediums fear for their lives if they are discovered. Many of my mentors, who have been practicing for more than 30 years, speak about the taboo nature of mediumship when they were in their earlier stages of development and just how much this has shifted.

So, why does mediumship matter? To understand just how profoundly powerful this practice is, contemplate first the cost of staying divided. Division is caused by fear. Fear happens where there is a lack of understanding. This occurs first within ourselves and ripples out to our families and friends, communities, countries, and our entire world. How good does deep division feel between loved ones and fellow citizens? How does it affect you and the way you are with yourself and others on a daily basis?

I was struggling, during a therapy session, with that feeling of exasperation and resentment about differing views between myself and other people in my country. On a conscious level, it was about differing beliefs, but then I decided I wanted to use the modality of EMDR, which stands for eye movement desensitization and reprocessing. One of the many mindblowing benefits of EMDR is its ability to help individuals gain a new and broader perspective on stressful situations and traumatic events.

When we finished, it became clear to me that under my anger and judgment of those who don't see the world through my eyes is the pain of being separate. I could see it with undeniable clarity.

Mediumship displays in real time the power of empathy, love, forgiveness, acknowledgement, validation, and the realization and awareness that we are all one. It's not to say that our earthly experience of division, fear, and hatred, is not a mandatory part of soul evolution. It is. How could we be pulled back toward our true selves—the spiritual aspect of us that resides within our human bodies—and in a way that requires significant soul growth, without having a life journey that includes our darker experiences.

Still, to put it plainly, mediumship reminds us of who we are and what really matters. It is a practice about the love that exists between us and the profound way in which we are all connected.

I brought through the deceased brother and mother of a sitter in a group reading. I was blown away by how transformed she was after she received messages from her passed loved ones about the heavy lifting she has done emotionally for others. She shared her response with me after the reading:

"In all my years of therapy I had not put together the grief (and guilt) my mother carried about Martin and how I tried to take care of that particular grief. I had only associated it with her sadness about my father's inability to be present. Her acknowledgement was incredible. I FELT her love and support and validation in a way that has released me from current struggles in relationships."

I've spoken with clients who've been able to release stress, anxiety, regret, fear, and grudges due to the messages they receive during a mediumistic reading. I had a client who was hardly speaking to her mother and an entire side of her family before her first reading with me. She received a message from her grandparents about her perspective about these family members that she told me was life-altering. The next time I read for her, she and her mother had moved in together and were living harmoniously. She had reached out to some relatives on that side of the family and offered what help she could while maintaining healthy boundaries. She seemed like a different person—and much more sure of herself.

Many spiritual practitioners believe that more people are becoming aware of their mediumistic gifts and that this spiritual awakening is meant to be a bridge for the division that we face. Whether you seek it because you hope to work professionally or you desire to create a deeper connection to Spirit and your higher self, you'll be creating more unity in your corner of the world and contributing peaceful energy. That matters. In the words of Mother Teresa, *"You cannot change the world, but you can cast a stone across the waters to create many ripples."*

03
Must-Knows For Approaching Mediumship Development

Even if you've read all the books, taken all the classes, and binge-watched YouTube videos of readings galore, the world of mediumship has so many unknowns and unanswered questions.

Often, when we discover our spiritual gifts, we have many questions, such as: Am I making this up because I've lost it, or am I communicating with a dead person? Should I be medicated and institutionalized, or does the world truly work in this magical way?

I can't tell you how many times a student has asked me, "Am I doing this right?" or, "Is this normal, or am making this up?" There are things I've wished I had known as I ventured into this mysterious and wondrous world of talking to the dead. Therefore, before we dive into my how-to system for developing as a medium, I'm sharing my perspective on things that might make your path more enjoyable and generally easier.

Can Anyone Learn to Become a Medium?

I believe that all humans have the innate ability to speak to Spirit on some level. I compare it to learning to play the piano. Anyone passionate about and willing to put the work into developing their skills as a pianist will no doubt be able to learn to play the piano to some level of proficiency. For some, this skill comes quickly and naturally. For others, developing a standard level of proficiency may be a slow and challenging process that takes much longer. Some people have a higher potential for the skill, and some may only take it so far, no matter how they strive.

I sometimes wonder what the world would be like if all humans were taught from a young age to speak to Spirit the way we learn to speak our native language. Would we find that many more of us are capable than we've realized? Would the world be a more peaceful, loving, and connected place? Would each of us have a deeper sense of self throughout our journey here on earth? Or is it vitally important that we arrive with a beginner's mind, forgetting where we've come from and what's possible? Is it meant to be that only some of us are passionately pulled toward the world of mediumship?

I'll always be curious about what that world might look like, but I firmly believe that venturing into our life journey with a beginner's mind is essential for the purpose of using this human experience to grow. I also feel that our earth experience is made to be a dissonant experience of good and bad, joy and sadness, excitement and anxiety, etc. Perhaps that is why we aren't all mediums.

How Long Does Mediumship Development Take?

Mediumship Development takes a lifetime for *everyone*. There isn't a time that arrives when you're done! It's important to understand this right from the beginning. There's no room for ego in mediumship. You will never think, *There's just nothing left for me to learn.*

When I hear a medium say they don't want to focus on the "beginner stuff" any longer, that's when I think to myself, *You're likely to get your ass handed to you, and soon.* If you want to understand how long it might take before you can give a quality reading and be consistent, that answer is a little more complicated.

Mediumship development is different for everyone because everyone reads in a very unique way that tends to match up with who they are as a person in their everyday life. If you have a lot of natural ability and a high potential, it's possible that you would develop more quickly than the average bear. For some reason, certain people seem to be what I call "quick studies." I consider myself a quick study, and I have a student who jumped into my beginner class as soon as she started to suspect she had mediumistic skills. Within twelve weeks, she was able to consistently identify the spirit coming through, present a substantial body of evidence that could be validated by her sitters, and deliver a message that affected her sitter in a positive way. By the end of the twelve-week class, she had enrolled in my advanced class and had continued to strengthen her skills substantially.

If you don't feel like mediumship comes easily to you or that you have a natural ability, your road to consistently giving high-quality readings may be a little longer. I was taking a class and spoke to a fellow medium who shared that she took classes for two years before she saw much progress at all. At the two year mark, things started to open up for her, but her progress was still significantly slower than my quick study student. Is this due to how you learn to develop your mediumship or the confidence you bring to your practice? Certainly those details make a lot of difference, and yet for reasons unknown to me, some people seem to come into their gifts much more quickly, or much more slowly. Regardless of your pace, if you commit to putting in the work consistently and continuously, there's no reason that you can't reach a certain level of proficiency.

Many tutors have shared with me that it took them years to consistently bring through a certain kind of evidence or that even after twenty to thirty years, they might not get names in every reading, for example. There are many mediums who have sat in a development circle for years before they gave readings publicly. A tutor at Arthur Findlay College once said to me, "I have people calling up about weekend-long courses we offer, asking if they'll be able to become a medium after the weekend is over. I tell them, 'No.'"

That doesn't mean that if you put the work in, you won't notice your skills growing. It's likely you will. While development can take a while, it doesn't mean that you won't be able to start bringing through powerful evidence—sometimes sooner than you think—even if delivering a full-fledged forty-five to sixty-minute reading with a high percentage of accuracy may not happen right away. And when you get to the point of advanced proficiency, I promise you that you'll have readings where you feel like you're flying and, every once in a while, a reading that confuses the shit out of you and may even have you biting your pillow through tears.

The good news? In my next chapter, I'll let you in on the system I use to teach mediumship development. I'll also share plenty of stories about students who saw their skills develop more quickly once they joined my circles and why I believe that is. One thing is for sure: The only way for you to know for certain how long development will take for you is to start practicing and doing the work with good support.

Your Mediumship Will Never Stay the Same

Depending on where you are in your development, I promise you that there will come a time, if you haven't experienced it already, where you realize that your mediumship isn't working in the same way it used to. When I first came into my gifts as a medium, I was completely dazzled and wowed by the Spirit World! They like to get you hooked by blowing your mind with things you might see, hear, feel, and sense in all kinds of ways.

My first sign that I was connecting with Spirit was the rapid beating of my heart along with epic amounts of excitement. Then one day, that cue wasn't happening quite the same anymore. Also at the beginning of my development, I received clairvoyant impressions often, meaning that I was seeing images in my mind's eye as a dominant means of communicating with spirits. I created a Spirit Shorthand Journal (that we'll discuss further along in this book), which is the practice of using symbols with Spirit and can help a medium to understand the meaning of an image much more quickly when its meaning is the same from reading to reading. Yup, I was a clairvoyant symbols girl and loving it. My other dominant clair at the time was clairaudience, meaning that I would often hear sounds, words, songs, or phrases in my thoughts that conveyed much of the information that a spirit would be telling me.

Soon enough I'd go through times–for a week or maybe two at most—where spirit communication would feel a little or *very* cloudy. Even when the day before or the reading before, impressions had been so clear. What was happening? Did I do something wrong? Was I losing my gift?

I called up a mentor of mine and asked her, "Is this normal? What's happening to me?" She laughed and said it was a normal part of progressing. She told me to imagine when I'm working and things are clear that I'm in a particular sized room, and once it's time for my gifts to grow, I have to walk through a hallway that's a little cloudy, but when I come out, I come into a much bigger room that is very clear and more expansive. That's how mediumship development cycles feel to me. How you work will constantly change and grow, but the quality of your readings will become higher and more consistent if you're putting in the effort.

One of the significant changes in my mediumship happened when I realized that I no longer had much time in between spiritual impressions, thoughts that are sent from Spirit. In many of my readings, I had no time to ask questions of the spirit. It often all came through without stopping, and I was no longer noticing which of the clair senses I was using to receive the information. For example, instead of seeing an image in my mind, then hearing a word or sound while getting a feeling about it or a sensation in the body and putting this string of thoughts together to understand the meaning, it felt like I was rattling off a story as quickly as possible and only hearing what I was saying once the words came out of my mouth! I had no time to think.

It's a little unnerving when you go through a change like this because you go from having built a solid foundation of trust in what you're receiving from Spirit to wondering if you're making everything up and going crazy all over again.

While it was the most significant change I'd experienced because my sitters continued to say "yes" and validate the information I was bringing through, I escaped a full-blown panic about what was going on and asked a mentor for her thoughts. She said something so helpful that I'll never forget.

She said, "As you become more and more precise with your mediumship, you blend more and more closely with Spirit. This is why so much of the information you receive will be claircognizant (clear-knowing). *The more you refine your craft, the less you will sense, and the more you will know.*"

I found myself wishing that someone had told me these things sooner! Perhaps I wouldn't have gotten my panties in a knot so much when I first experienced my mediumship changing and evolving. Now when my mediumship shifts I just say to myself, "Great, I'm getting an upgrade!"

Psychic Versus Mediumistic

A lot of new mediums want to skip over working psychically and go straight to chatting with people six feet under. I get it. If I'm honest, I was pretty excited about that aspect as well. I caution you, though, that is most definitely a mistake.

First, let's discuss the difference between working psychically and working mediumistically. When you work psychically, you are not speaking to a deceased spirit. Instead, you're blending with the energetic aura of a living person (or thing). All living people and things have an energetic field surrounding them that we call the aura. This energetic field, or aura, is said to store information from lifetimes upon lifetimes. To read what's in the aura, you use your clair senses. The psychic field is also at a certain vibration that is lower than when working mediumistically.

When you're working mediumistically, you are connecting with Spirit at that higher vibration. This means you are not connecting with the energetic field of a living person or thing, but with the energy of the deceased spirit. To receive this information, you use the clair senses.

You may have noticed that you use your clair senses to receive information whether you're working psychically or mediumistically. Why is this so important? You can get a lot of the same information about a passed spirit from the aura of a living person. That means that if you tell someone who is getting a reading from you that their loved one is present, but you're simply getting the information from the aura of your client, that what you've said isn't true, and it's simply unethical. The problem is, not all mediums have been trained to know the difference. It's common for a beginning medium to be giving information (what we call evidence) from a spirit, and then when they start relaying a message from the spirit to have actually dropped down to the psychic vibration and be reading from the aura without knowing it.

If you want to work professionally and ethically, you must know the difference and be proficient at both. You are always advancing your mediumship when you work psychically because you are working to strengthen the language that is used for both psychic work and mediumistic work.

Mediumship Ethics

Our job as mediums is to deliver clear and accurate pieces of evidence and a message from a spirit to our sitter. The purpose of this is to provide a healing and positive experience for them, and above all, to do no harm. Discovering your skills as a medium is a very exciting, and sometimes a lonely, isolating, or nerve-wracking time too. New mediums are usually looking for just about any piece of validation they can find to give them proof that their experiences are real.

That means that we come into this new world wanting to use our gifts in all kinds of ways to figure out what the hell is going on. *Sometimes,* unfortunately, it's unknowingly at the expense of other people when a new medium isn't aware or informed of mediumship ethics. While I could write an entire book on the subject, I'm sharing some of the most important ethical practices to be aware of so you're not an accidental douche canoe.

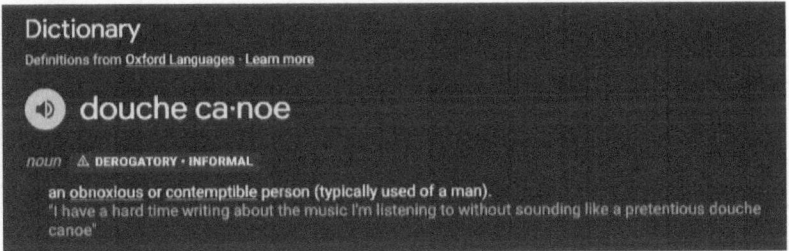

1) Never give a reading without both consent and education!

I'm sure you've seen TV series or shows about mediums where a stranger is approached by the medium and given a reading. At best in these situations, the medium asks quickly for permission from the unassuming and often very surprised person, who generally happens to be in a public space. Not cool, and here's why.

While these moments are often shown in a positive light and can turn out well, there is always a strong chance that this will go awry at the expense of the person being read. We never know the state of a stranger. Are they going through a rough time in life where they are emotionally vulnerable and fragile? Did the spirit who wants to come through cause them trauma or abuse them? Are they in a private enough space to be able to take in the reading? Consider that readings can get really personal really quick and often bring up strong emotions. My sitters cry in the vast majority of my readings, not to mention that sometimes, information can come through quite quickly and feel like *a lot* for the person receiving. Maybe your sitter is having a great day or is in a wonderful chapter of life and the reading shifts them away from that great day by bringing up emotions they weren't ready to deal with. After all, the purpose of mediumship is to provide catharsis and healing and, often, the facing of emotions or relationship dynamics—and becoming aware of belief systems are all a part of that. This is why not just consent, but also education is so important. Many people you come into contact with in the world don't have a thorough understanding of the practice of mediumship, if they have any at all! That means if you ask if they'd like to hear from their passed loved ones, they'll likely say yes without the true knowledge of what type of experience they are saying yes to.

I like to let my clients know that sitting with a medium has some level of risk. You may hear inaccurate information for any number of reasons, even from a good medium, that may affect you. A medium's words can have a powerful effect on a sitter for better or for worse. This is why it's so important to work with a medium who understands the responsibility that we undertake. I always explain a bit about how mediumship works and what to expect. I additionally describe how I work specifically, since every medium is different, and how sitters can advocate for themselves at any time if the information touches upon something sensitive or doesn't seem to make sense to them.

2) You're not a doctor, therapist, counselor, here to give advice or provide coaching.

So don't act like it. First, Spirit is the entity speaking, not you. Additionally, Spirit will not tell someone to sell the house, get divorced, buy a lottery ticket, etc. Spirit understands even better than we do that solving your problems for you robs you of the life experience you came here for.

If someone comes to you for a mediumship reading, give them that service, and do not assume the profession of another practitioner when you are not qualified. People come to mediums emotionally vulnerable much of the time. Some of them likely require the help of a therapist or coach. Have a list of practitioners you can refer them to. Even if you *are* a practicing therapist or doctor, stick to what they came to you for and set up another time for a different service. I am not a medical medium, and I understand that mediums of this nature may help identify diseases and such. If this is the case for you, make sure you work with a legitimate legal professional to understand how to practice safely for both you and your clients.

3) Focus on evidence that can be validated by your sitter.

I'm all about Evidential Mediumship. This practice focuses on bringing through information about and messages from a passed loved one in spirit that provides confirmation to our sitter that this spirit is present. That means that the things you share can be validated by your sitter. Evidence such as their personality and character, their cause of passing, gender identity, relationship and role to the sitter, marital status, pets, hobbies, name, etc., and a message that makes sense can all be confirmed by the person receiving the reading. I have most definitely received wild information from the other side that cannot be validated. For example, I sometimes have deceased spouses give permission for their living spouse to move on romantically, and that cannot actually be proven, can it? However, my readings are 95% chock-full of things that can, and usually when I share these other tidbits, my sitter will feel that these things that often come through during the message aspect of the reading make perfect sense to them.

4) Avoid negative or fearful predictions.

I haven't had a single person come to me for a reading because they wanted to get bad news. I haven't met anyone who felt like hearing about negative premonitions or predictions helped them live a better life. The thing about predictions is that even if you are correct, things *change*! There are also plenty of times when bad things happen, but we have no control over them. The real question is, what is the value added? If someone is looking to be diagnosed with a medical condition, they can visit a suitable practitioner or medical medium, if that's in their comfort zone. Sitters can get nervous even when you don't share anything scary, so take responsibility for the effect that your words have on your clients. I really believe that if troubles and challenges are meant to come to pass, they will, so use your work to share truths that lend themselves to your client living a better, more honest, more fulfilling life!

5) Ask permission to continue if sensitive information comes up and keep in mind the setting of the reading.

Just because Spirit is sharing something doesn't mean that you just blurt it out without preparing your sitter and asking permission if it feels quite heavy or private, especially if you're in a group setting. When approaching a subject that feels iffy, like sexual abuse, a gruesome death, or infidelity, I usually say something like this, "Your wife is bringing up information that some people consider to be private regarding their cause of passing or relationship dynamics. Are you comfortable if I continue to share what they have to say?" Even as you are connecting with Spirit, be aware of the state of your sitter and their comfort level.

6) Their loved ones are likely not cursed nor are they stuck between worlds.

Never during a reading has Spirit communicated information like this to me. I don't deny that evil entities or all kinds of things and energy that I am unaware of may very well exist, but often I hear of this being shared when a medium or psychic is inviting a client to come back for sessions continuously to "break a curse" or "try again" to contact a loved one.

7) Keep your bias out of the reading. Work instead to be a clear channel.

This comes with practice, but it's good to be aware from the beginning that it's ever so easy to make assumptions while giving a reading, especially when you're just getting started. Remember that people are nuanced and complex. You're not reading a spirit who was simply a grumpy or happy person. People have all kinds of sides to them, and often when you read for a different friend or family member that knows the same spirit, you will be surprised just how different the reading plays out. Once you start bringing through evidence, it's easy to decide with your brain that you've *heard this kind of story before*, but never make assumptions. I once read for a mother and daughter, bringing through the mother's husband, who was also the daughter's dad. He was an upstanding guy with a good sense of humor, missed deeply, etc. A few months later, I read for a different daughter, bringing through the same father in spirit. In this reading, he expressed apologies and acknowledgment of the effect he'd had on his daughter due to alcoholism and drug abuse. I couldn't believe it was the same person. It turned out, this sister was 12 years younger than the other daughter and that the father hadn't dealt with addiction until his older children had turned 18 and moved out. We often fall prey to painting our own experiences onto a spirit because we all work from our own frame of reference. I share with all of my students that I get regular energy work and do weekly therapy to leave my baggage and bias behind in my readings for the cleanest experience possible for my sitter.

8) Offer a refund or to reschedule if the reading doesn't work out.

I will repeat this multiple times throughout this book; be prepared to have a shitstorm reading from time to time, even once you reach a level of high proficiency as a medium. Remember that there are so many unknown factors you don't have control over, such as the energy of your sitter and how they show up or the way that the passed spirit chooses to communicate with you. Remember also that your mediumship constantly changes as you progress. You'll receive information in new kinds of ways, and sometimes it may seem cloudy or unfamiliar. That's right, Spirit keeps you on your toes! I promise you that you'll be flying high with many fantastic readings under your belt. Then, unfortunately, you'll find yourself utterly confused after a reading where all you hear is, "No, I don't understand what you're saying." It happens to everyone, and any medium who tells you otherwise is full of it. Simple as that. When it happens, handle it by offering R&R, baby. Offer to reschedule if they weren't a nightmare to read for or to refund them if they were unpleasant. I give every sitter either choice and allow them to email me their answer later if they feel uncomfortable making a decision on the spot. After all, it's a super bummer for anyone who is excited about hearing from their loved ones to experience a botched reading that doesn't work out. This is also a great way to take pressure off of you as a medium. You have a backup plan if, for any reason, you can't deliver the service you promised.

My Take on Negative Spirits and Dark Energy

I have not experienced negative spirits or dark energy. I couldn't say whether they exist or not. There is certainly both evil and good that exists in human form, so perhaps it makes sense that both exist in the spiritual realm as well. For me, this ties into my spiritual boundaries, which I dive deeper into in chapter twenty-nine about mediumship maintenance and best practices. I have no doubt that if dark energy or negative spirits exist that I'm not a person they'd come to mingle with as I have no interest or availability whatsoever. For me, my belief system and boundary around this is a built in "protection," if you will.

In the same best practices chapter that I referenced, I'll additionally discuss my simple method of protecting my energy prior to working with Spirit. While I do say a prayer before I give readings, I use it to be clear about my intentions. My protection practices are not extensive by any means. If my prayer and intention works as protection from dark entities too, that's lovely, and I'll take it.

Additionally, I do my own version of energetically cleansing my space from time to time when I feel inclined. I do this to release any extra energy that isn't mine and because I feel that it helps me to take good care of my nervous system. I keep this really simple. I don't perform any long rituals or use many tools. Sometimes it looks like lifting energy from my feet to my hips while I breath quickly and then doing a forward bend and imagining it all falling off and being swept away out the window. Other times I'll wash my hands and imagine all of the energy that isn't mine washing away. Another favorite of mine is turning on the fan in my office and seeing all of the extra energy being swept away and out of the room.

I've met many mediums, and there are always belief systems that we share and those that differ. I recommend establishing practices that make you feel secure and comfortable when you work with Spirit.

Don't Let Anyone Put Limitations on You As a Medium

With all of the unknowns and unanswered questions about mediumship, how can any of us say what is or isn't possible when it comes to Spirit communication? Some mediums give spiritual assessments where they provide clarity to you about your unfolding gifts. These types of readings should be realistic but also provide encouragement. The person who knows you and your mediumship best is you. Who you are as a person and as a medium is a journey for you to take. I do believe that if you feel a strong pull and passion toward this work, there is likely a reason. Maybe it's not about becoming a professional medium or even giving readings regularly. Perhaps instead, it's about developing your relationship with Spirit. Whatever the case, that's for you to discover. What can hurt from following where this path leads you, as long as you use what you learn for good? So please, don't let anyone tell you what you aren't capable of or what isn't possible for you.

You're Not On This Journey Alone

Just know that you're not on this path alone. You've got this book in your hands, and we'll be going on quite the journey together! You're not the first person to be overwhelmed, delighted, and freaked out by Spirit, among other things. If you feel lonely and isolated on your journey because of where you live or people in your life who don't understand, you aren't the first.

There are more fellow humans than you might realize who are on the mediumship path, perhaps even looking for community or a friend like you. What's more, we are so incredibly fortunate to be living in a time where very few of us feel afraid for our lives by sharing that we talk to dead people. There are classes you can join and people you can meet who will resonate with your story and experiences. If this is just the beginning for you, I couldn't be more honored.

I promise you that even if you don't feel you have support here on earth, or even if you do, that you have oodles of support from the other side in the form of guides, angels, and more. I'll be diving into the idea of creating a community in a future chapter that I promise you don't want to miss. Until then, know that you are guided and supported like a motherfucker.

04
My Mediumship Development Framework

It's easy to fall into the pattern of plateauing in your mediumship. Maybe you've been to a mediumship class or development circle before, only to continue to lack confidence in the same old things like: efficiently identifying the spirit(s), also known as anchoring the link; keeping the energy up when you hear "*no*" from your sitter; getting specific evidence; using symbols effectively; conveying the message; and more. Here's the thing. A clair exercise here or there may give you a nudge forward, but to truly advance as a medium, you must be working through the full mechanics of mediumship that can help you to expand your awareness and continue to strengthen your connection with Spirit.

In my previous business, I constantly reminded my clients that it's not just information that gets results. It's the organization and implementation of information that gets results. I have found this to be true no matter what I'm looking to create in life, and mediumship is no different. I feel that since it can be so elusive, having a system becomes even more paramount.

Whether I'm focused on teaching others or working on my own development, I use my *__Mediumship Development Framework__*.

If you're ever heard the phrase "structure creates freedom," that's the purpose of my framework. It provides the structure to support your development in the most efficient way, yet the freedom and spontaneity to avoid being put in a box—so that you can discover the special and unique way that *you* work.

As you work on and strengthen each of the 5 Cs that my framework focuses on, you'll strengthen your rapport with and your connection to the Spirit World. Continuously working with this framework will give you the tools to develop each of the Cs in your own unique way that is in integrity with who you uniquely are as a medium, and as a person.

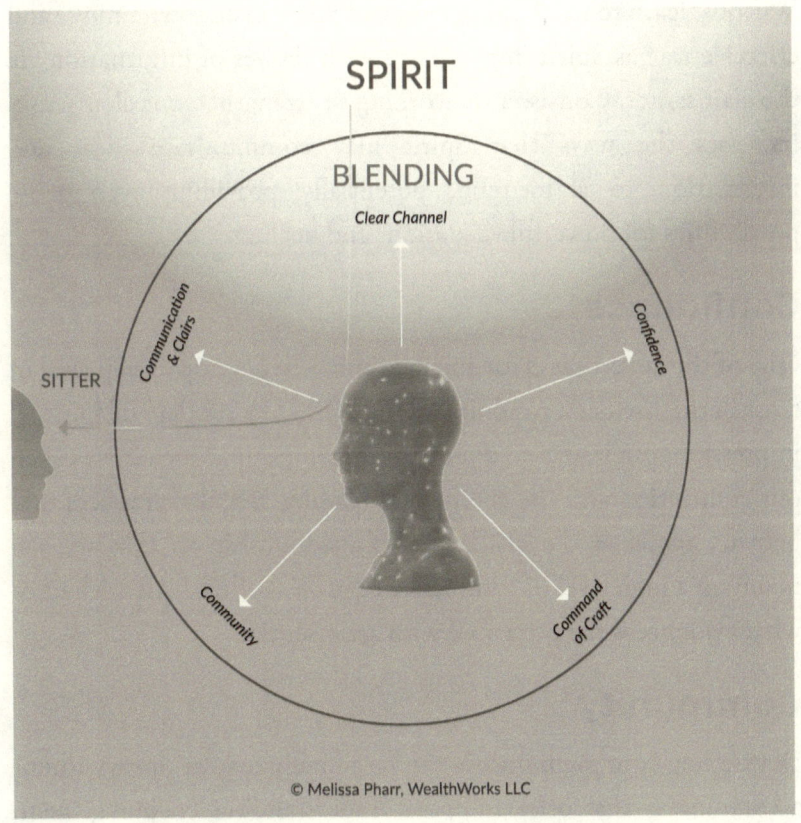

© Melissa Pharr, WealthWorks LLC

Clear Channel

As conduits between the physical world and the Spirit World, our mediumship becomes more accurate and unbiased when we increase our ability to become the clearest channel possible. Meditation and Sitting in the Power are some examples of practices and exercises that help to calm, relax, clear, and expand the awareness of the mind for quality spirit communication.

Communication and the Clairs

We must learn to speak the language of Spirit in our own unique and effective way as Spirit impresses us with flashes of information via the clair senses. Consistently working to strengthen our clair senses increases the ways that Spirit may communicate ideas and information to a medium, potentially providing even more possibilities for powerful validations and healing.

Confidence

One of the largest tasks for any medium is to develop a deep level of trust in themselves as a conduit and in Spirit. The subtlety of spiritual impressions can lead us to doubt our mediumship, which can weaken our connection and the energy of a reading. Regular practices that help us adapt to the challenges of mediumship so that we can maintain a high level of confidence regardless of who sits with us or what evidence we're presented with are essential.

Community

Developing your mediumship can be a lonely road at times without a community that offers support, understanding, encouragement, and friendship. Having a place to practice, to ask for help, to receive inspiration and encouragement, and to be given direction when needed can be a significant part of advancing your mediumship.

Command of Craft

A combination of continuous practice using your skills and focused, targeted steps toward improving your abilities to expand your mediumistic toolbox can help you progress more efficiently. Doing readings on a regular basis and identifying an area of your mediumship that you'd like to focus on improving over a decided timeline can be a powerful way to move forward in your mediumship.

Throughout the following chapters, I'll be diving deep into each of these 5 Cs within my Mediumship Development Framework. My clients know that I hold nothing back and that I love getting into the nitty-gritty details that often make all the difference when it comes to finally feeling confident about an aspect of your mediumship and your practice in general. I'll share behind the scenes stories from my own development journey and stories about the journeys of my students, plus more.

05
Becoming a Clear Channel

A medium who is working at their best is merely an empty vessel through which spirits speak. If you've ever practiced meditation, you may already have an understanding of clearing your mind and finding that stillness that is required. One of the many challenges that most people face when they practice meditation is their own thoughts getting in their way. The same can be said with the practice of mediumship. When a medium receives information from a spirit, a common question to ask, especially at the beginning of development is, "Am I making this up, or is this information from a spirit?" A thought that your brain thinks can sometimes get in the way. How do we overcome that? How does a medium tell the difference between a thought from our own mind and a thought that is being communicated from Spirit?

A thought from a spirit, or a spiritual impression, as we call it, will likely feel as if it's just dropped into your head. It won't feel as if it was simply the next logical thought for your brain. It also doesn't tend to be connected to your own personal recent thoughts or experiences or assumptions you might make because of your own unique life experience. When it's super obvious that it's from Spirit, you'll say, "I know *that* thought was nowhere in my head a moment ago!" because in no way is it recognizable as a thought of yours. Things can get a bit more complex as you develop. Spirit will most definitely give information in an intelligent order that makes sense and shapes a powerful story throughout a reading. As you become highly proficient, spiritual impressions will come faster and even move into more of a flow state. The good news is that by then, the difference will have likely become more pronounced for you. This comes with time and experience.

But being a Clear Channel isn't just about being able to clear your mind. It's also about cleaning up your emotional and mental baggage and developing yourself. Spirit works off of our frame of reference. That means that our memories and experiences are of great use to them and that they will use what we know from our life experience to get across any piece of evidence or message. The more emotional baggage we carry around that colors our life experience, the more likely that the message we share or the way we interpret the evidence we receive may be biased. Our own experiences and understanding of the world make it easy to make assumptions in our interpretations of spiritual impressions. For some of us, being a Clear Channel may also be affected by foods we eat, the things we drink, and our overall environment. The best place to start? Learn what levers you can pull to help you become the clearest channel possible!

Meditation

One of the most powerful and important practices that you can begin on your own is the practice of meditation. If I'm honest, I spent most of my life despising the idea of meditation, but after a while, it called to me. I started small and eventually grew to crave the time that I spend in silence. Meditation is the simple practice of quieting your mind and bringing your body into a peaceful and relaxed state. I'm sure there are all kinds of ways that we could make it more complicated, but why? I like to look at it as time to recharge and to go within. In the beginning, I very much struggled with thinking I was meditating "wrong" because thoughts would enter my mind while I was trying to quiet it. I've found, though, that what you resist persists. I let any thoughts that enter during meditation simply float on by. If I feel anxious or stressed about remembering certain thoughts that come to mind, I'll keep a notepad next to me and write them down. These thoughts subside once I get them out of my head and onto paper. The simple practice that I and many people use to create the quiet is focusing on our breath. I don't worry about counting my breath cycles, controlling the pace of my breath, or anything of the sort. I bring my attention to my breath, refocusing as needed, and before I know it, twenty minutes have flown by.

Meditation Exercise

Sit in a comfortable position. I like to kneel on the floor and place two yoga blocks under my butt. Sometimes I also sit on a yoga bolster with my hips propped up higher than my ankles and feet. Find whatever position works best for you. Put a timer on for any amount of time that feels doable for you. I started my meditation practice with just three to five minutes on my timer. Bring your attention to your breath. For three breath cycles, just observe your breathing without trying to control it. Then bring your attention to your exhale. Think of this exhale as a cleansing breath that releases any thoughts and worries from your mind and any tension from your body. Imagine your shoulders relaxing further with every exhale. If thoughts enter your mind, don't resist them; just let them float on by. Continue to refocus your mind on your breath. If it helps to focus only on your exhale, try that. If you'd like to keep a journal next to you to record any new insights or fleeting thoughts that are pestering you, do it. This may be helpful to allow you to release your active mind and get into a deeper state of meditation. If you still struggle to get through this time quieting your mind, perhaps you can listen to instrumental music that is calming or even follow a guided meditation.

Sitting in the Power

What exactly *is* sitting in the power? First, it's not the same thing as meditation, which is about going within and recharging as you quiet your mind. While sitting in the power helps you to quiet your mind and to become a clear channel as well, it is instead about going outward with your energy and expanding it. Sitting in the power is sometimes called Sitting with Spirit. It focuses on the skill of making a subtle shift to connect with the energy of Spirit.

Why is this so important? Without making that mediumistic shift and building the power as you blend with the Spirit World, mediumship simply isn't possible. While you may still receive impressions, if there is no mediumistic shift and power built, you'll be reading intuitively instead of connecting with Spirit.

During a session of sitting in the power (SIP), we practice two aspects of getting in touch with that energy. First, you become familiar with the experience of sitting with your own spirit. For me, when I first begin, I focus on imaging my energy expanding outside of my body in the form of light, so that the spaces around me grow brighter. I also imagine that my spirit pulls just slightly away from my body and sits just in front of me as I sit with it peacefully. Second, you become familiar with the experience of blending your energy with the energy of the Spirit World. When I blend with the energy of the Spirit World, I imagine a blanket of energy or light, or sometimes even the feeling of love pouring over me. If I remind myself to relax on the exhale of my breath and expand my energy on the inhale of my breath, my body will begin to feel lighter, and sometimes I'll no longer feel aware of my body. It's as if I'm suspended and am floating somewhere off in the energy of Spirit.

Other sensations I feel as the Spirit World draws near is the heat of my body intensifying or that I'm breathing thicker, steamier air. When I connect with Spirit during a SIP session or while giving a reading, the presence of a spirit or the Spirit World feels very much like someone is standing next to me on my right side, but I can only see them as a silhouette in my mind.

Practicing these two parts is paramount. You must learn to recognize the energy of your own spirit so that you can know the difference when another spirit blends with you. The SIP practice helps you develop your ability not just to shift into a mediumistic state, but to sit with that spiritual power and to build that power. When you are building the power, this is the building of that subtle spiritual energy that you become accustomed to.

I remember when I was first wrapping my mind around this concept of SIP that it didn't feel quite clear. I had a hard time understanding WTF these spiritual weirdos were talking about, if I'm honest. What was this *subtle shift*? What was their definition of *power*? One reason I hesitate to put too many descriptions in place for you is due to the fact that every medium experiences SIP, and Spirit, differently. Some say they feel the sensations of having cobwebs on their face or someone playing with their hair. Strange, huh? Others feel their bodies heat up or cool down.

If you don't feel many sensations, or any at all, as you begin, don't worry! If you have trouble imagining the expansion of your energy or feeling the subtle sensations of your own spirit or the Spirit World, just trust and *know* that it's happening. While I know that feels a little like bullshit, just go with it. You have to spend time allowing yourself to attune to the practice and its subtleties, but I promise that if you stick with it, the experience will begin to feel familiar and understood.

My students ask me how they should approach their time SIP. Is there something they should expect to happen during their SIP sessions? The best advice I can give you is to go in with no expectations of sparkling paranormal experiences or strange and miraculous happenings. The Spirit World is eager to work with you, and they will do their work during your sitting sessions whether you notice or not. I like to keep things simple, and I set the intention before I sit so that the Spirit World will use this time to help me further develop my mediumship. Yup, that's it.

All aspects of mediumship become more elusive when you pile high expectations on an experience that is instead most powerful when you are as present as possible in the moment. It seems the more I approach SIP and mediumship in general in this way, the more I am wowed by unexpected and beautiful experiences.

I know right now you're also wondering if SIP is a great time to get in touch with your spirit guides, or whether you *should* be aware of them or not as you develop mediumistically? I'll talk more about spirit guides further on in this book, but for now, just know that being aware of your guides is in no way a requirement for SIP to be effective. While there are SIP guided experiences that include meeting with your guides, in no way is that the most important aspect of sitting in and building mediumistic power. In addition, let me just say that in my experience, your guides will make you aware of them when necessary.

Sitting In The Power Exercise

Focus first on your breath for three breath cycles. Now bring your attention to your exhale.

With each exhale, imagine your body relaxing. With each exhale, imagine your energy feeling open to this experience, but without pressure or expectation. Allow yourself to be present in each moment. As you continue to bring your attention to your exhale, scan your body from head to toe, allowing yourself to move more deeply into a state of relaxation.

Now, bring your attention to the true essence of you—your spirit. Notice the sensations you feel, however subtle, of connecting to your own spirit. Enjoy this feeling of being home.

And now, with each inhale, without effort, sense the energy of your spirit expanding out and up.

It is filling the space that you are in, and with each inhale, the energy of your spirit effortlessly grows beyond the space that you are in and out into nature. With each exhale, your body continues to relax. Continue connecting with the energy of your own spirit as you feel it expand and you feel your vibration lift. Enjoy this feeling of sitting with your own spirit for a few minutes.

And now, imagine a bright, white, point of light high above you and off to one side. The light begins to grow and shine down, circling you. Feel the warmth of this light as it covers you.

And know that this is the light of the Spirit World surrounding you. Feel the feeling of love that comes with this light of the Spirit World. Notice the sensations you feel as this light comes to blend with your own. Focus your attention on the blending of your spirit with the light of the Spirit World. Notice how strong the blend feels to you and how peaceful it feels to be connected.

Now, sit and enjoy this feeling for a while without expectation or pressure.

Sit for at least five minutes.

Now it's time to bring yourself back to your physical reality in the space where you sit, knowing you can always come back at any time. Thank the Spirit World for spending this time with you. Bring your attention back to your breath. Begin to become aware of your fingers and toes. Begin to become aware of your entire body. When you are ready, open your eyes and continue on with your day. Do your best to practice SIP regularly, perhaps three times a week for 20 minutes.

For more SIP guided sessions and meditations, visit my YouTube channel SIP playlist using the QR code:

Self-Development and Emotional Health

My best teachers have acknowledged how closely tied self development (and our emotional health) and mediumship actually are. Truly, for us to significantly progress as mediums, we must continue to move forward with a deepening understanding of ourselves and the things about ourselves that we need to work on in order to live happier and more peaceful lives. Why? Think about yourself in relationship with you and others. When we have lots of emotional triggers and baggage that hasn't been dealt with, patterns reveal themselves all over the place in our relationships, and whether we'd like to admit it or are even aware of it, *we* are the common denominator. For example, have you ever had a friend who bounces from relationship to relationship? Perhaps the partners they date are similar to each other, or maybe they're not. Regardless, one thing remains constant, your friend tends to play the same role, and things tend to end the same way, which means the relationships don't work out. Your friend is stuck in a cycle or a pattern that leads them to repeat frustrating experiences, and they are the common denominator.

What's for certain is that our experiences with ourselves and others are not as easy as they might be without shedding those triggers, behaviors, and baggage that keep us stuck repeating patterns or seeing certain situations with the same bias. The same is true for mediumship. As mediums, we're telling the stories of spirits who once lived as humans among their loved ones. When our emotional and mental state is clear, we can view information and tell stories more honestly, without the bias.

I was teaching a class in my mediumship development circle the other week, and my students were practicing photo reading. The person in the photo had struggled with severe anxiety, and some of my students were able to identify this fact, while a few others were not. One of the students who didn't mention anxiety as a piece of her evidence told me that she had felt a lot of anxiety but hadn't shared that as part of her evidence because she just assumed it was her own. I said to her, "I could tell you weren't feeling that anxiety when the reading began." She agreed, and confirmed she had been completely calm. "Then why," I asked, "would you assume it was yours and not his? You were well connected to this spirit, but you didn't trust what he was sharing with you because of your own tendency to experience anxiety."

This is not to say that this student should be anxiety-free to be an exceptional medium. It is to point out that the more aware we are of ourselves and our own tendencies, and the more we are able to separate ourselves from the stories and situations of others, the more honest we will be as people and mediums, making far less assumptions about others during a reading and in our life.

There is no right or wrong way to do this as long as you have support and do the work that gets you results. I share openly with my students that for me, *seeing a therapist* on a regular basis has been life changing. As we go through life, we all take emotional hits and endure challenging experiences that cause us to struggle, to question, and hopefully, to ultimately grow. The same way I like to exercise my body for my physical health on a regular basis, I do the work regularly to take care of my emotional and mental health, and damn is it worth it. The other support I get every few months or once a quarter is *seeing an energy worker.* There's a whole slew of different kinds of energy workers, and the best way to find one is to ask for referrals. Mediumship is all about working with energy, so to me it makes a lot of sense to have someone move mine around and clean it up. I can't say I know exactly how this works, but I know I see major results in terms of my behavior with myself and others. I have better relationships than ever before, and I feel much more self aware, like I'm carrying a lot less on my shoulders. As I move into reading more from the stage for large groups, I can guarantee you that the minute I walk offstage, I'll head straight to an energy worker to clear, cleanse, and replenish my energy after working so hard with energy and potentially taking on energy that isn't mine.

Maybe these modalities aren't what calls to you most in terms of your emotional health and self development. That's ok. Maybe journaling helps you, or tapping, or breathwork, or any combination of practices that help us in terms of our self development. What's important is to find your way and reap the benefits of better mediumship, not to mention a happier life.

Self-Development and Emotional Health Exercise

Take some time to sit with yourself in a peaceful and quiet place. Reflect on who you've become as a person at this point in your life.

1. Describe your own personality and character.
2. Make a list of ten ways that you've grown as a person so far and are most proud of.
3. Make a list of ten ways that you'd like to grow as a person still.
4. Brainstorm five ideas about what support you might need to grow in these ways.

Physical Health

Another important aspect of being a clear channel is our physical health, but by no means have I found by observing mediums that you have to be perfectly fit or have it all sorted out. I've witnessed mediums in pretty poor states of health give tremendous readings. With all of these different levers that you can pull to become a clearer channel, you'll have to discover the combination that works best for you. Throughout my life, I have had a body that is sensitive to the things I eat and drink and to how I care for it. I've found that this carries over into my mediumship. Before becoming pregnant with my second child, I did a clean-eating plan for about three months and I was *wowed* by how much clearer spiritual impressions came to me. It felt so much easier to give a reading, and my accuracy was at a high level. That being said, I've had times when I've been pretty darn sick with a cold or have eaten foods my body doesn't like and still managed to give great readings. I've also been just barely functioning with morning sickness and unable to focus enough to work.

Our physical health is an area that each of us really need to play with to see what tends to matter the most. I do my best to avoid dairy, gluten, sugar, and alcohol on a regular basis because I feel great when I do and pretty horrible when I don't. I've seen the wonders it does for me as a medium, so I have pretty strong incentives. I understand though that for some people, staying away from these things is not a happy thought.

Physical movement is another important lever for me to pull. Throughout my life, I've always been at my best mentally, emotionally, and physically when I am regularly active and moving and strengthening my body. You might guess that for me, this also strengthens my mediumship and helps me with keeping my energy grounded after giving lots of readings. I find in so many ways that the things that serve us day to day in our life show up similarly in our mediumship, whether it be our style as a medium or the levers that are most uniquely important for us to pull in order for us to do our best work. No matter where you are in your development, do consider once again that our bodies are our vessels, and whatever will support them to be the cleanest and clearest they can be on any and every level will likely benefit us not just in life but as mediums. I often feel excited and inspired to try out different changes for one to three months at a time and see if I notice improvements in my readings.

Physical Health Exercise

Reflect on how you care for yourself physically. Imagine what it would be like to feel physically great before every reading you give. How might this change your readings?

1. Do you feel like movement or regular exercise could shift your mediumship? What might that look like?
2. Do you feel like eating different foods could shift your mediumship? What might that look like?

3. Do you feel that what you drink could shift your mediumship? What might that look like?
4. List any changes you feel inspired to make in terms of how you manage your physical health.

Decluttering

There is now substantial evidence that an organized physical environment promotes cognitive function, a positive mood, and the reduction of stress. I've spoken to people who feel strongly that their environment and the organization and cleanliness of it is paramount to their performance as a medium. I care greatly about my environment in the same way, but I also have two small children, so clutter and chaos is a natural and unpreventable part of my life at times. I can give an incredible reading in a pretty messy office, but I have my limits. Our home is put in order at the end of every week to start Mondays off well, and any person in my family will tell you that I start to lose it if I'm living in what feels like a pit for too long. Many mediums practice different rituals for the right feel in their space, especially before and after they read. For me, I like an organized office space where I can conduct my work and readings, but I'm not one for ritual or anything that takes me much longer than thirty seconds to a couple of minutes before a reading. I promise you there will be experiences where you don't have much time for those things before you're asked to work, and I personally feel that for many, they are a crutch and a belief system of what someone "needs" beforehand in order to do their best work.

Decluttering Exercise

Evaluate your physical space, especially the space where you tend to give readings. How does it feel to you?

1. Shift, organize, declutter, or clean your physical space where you give readings, and see how it feels to you afterward. Does this make a difference for you?
2. If you feel inspired, shift, organize, declutter, or clean another physical space in your home, and see how it feels to you afterward.

06
Communication and the Clairs

Suddenly the image of a beach ball dropped into my mind. It was entirely plain looking and sitting alone on a sandy beach. I took a breath as I studied this ball. Then, "Your mom is showing me a beach ball right now. That's funny." I smiled as I continued to hold the image in my mind. My sitter was silent, but a slight smile spread over her face.

Next, I heard the word "vacation." It came in quickly and was accompanied by an overwhelming feeling of deep gratitude and the kind of love that pours out of your heart so fully that you feel like you could sob heavily with happy tears while holding a person you love. The next word I heard was what so clearly pulled this string of thoughts beautifully together that this spirit was sending me: "Philippines."

I was sensing it all at once now as the meaning poured into my mind in what felt like a flash. I looked up at my sitter, "Your mom says you're going on vacation to the Philippines with your family. You're bringing your sons so they can know more about her home country and their culture."

My sitter began to wipe tears from her eyes. The feeling was so strong I spoke in first person, "Thank you for taking them. I thought you didn't care about your culture and where you came from. I know

now that I was wrong, and I was scared about you losing this part of yourself." My sitter nodded as she wept and smiled, a deeper understanding coming over her about her mother and their relationship.

Mediumship is the practice of being able to speak to Spirit so that you can relay powerful messages to those still living to help them move forward in life. In order to do that, we have to learn the language of Spirit, and we do this by using our clair senses. As we dive into learning about the clair senses, we also need to have an understanding of how spirit communication actually works, so let's start there.

Most mediums work subjectively when they are giving mediumistic readings. That means that Spirit communicates with them through thought, as this mother in spirit did when she told me about my sitter's upcoming family vacation. The best way to describe it is that it feels very similar to paying attention to a daydream. That's not to say that many mediums haven't experienced Spirit objectively. When you experience Spirit objectively, it means that you are sensing Spirit outside of your thoughts and body, as you would sense anything or anyone else with your five senses as a living person. Some people report seeing a spirit, hearing noises or voices, or smelling the perfume of a past loved one. If you've had objective experiences with Spirit, excellent! Still, most mediums, when they say something like, "Your mom is showing me a beachball," as I did, are sensing these impressions subjectively. Moving forward, assume that as we discuss Communication and the Clairs, we are describing subjective communication.

You already know that when a spirit sends a thought to you and it drops into your mind, we call this a *spiritual impression*. Spirit is impressing you with a thought. This thought can come via any one of the clair senses or even a combination of them. When they come in combination, this is the same way that you use your five senses as a living person in conjunction with each other. For example, you *see* your friend waving goodbye, *hear* them saying, "See you next time!" and *feel* sadness that they are leaving but gratitude that you got time with them. As you are just beginning in mediumship, you may experience a spiritual impression via only one of the clair senses at a time, but as you progress, you'll use your clair senses more often in conjunction with each other. You might have noticed this as I described myself first seeing the beach ball, but then also hearing different words, "vacation" and "Philippines" and feeling strong emotions as the meaning behind the message began to unfold.

Although spiritual impressions come one thought at a time, as you develop your mediumship, the speed at which they come may increase. It's like learning any new skill. You may have to take it slow when you begin. Just one impression at a time, but as you get better, you might experience them flowing in more quickly. I remember when I was beginning. I would get an image or hear a word and then take a bit of time to lean into the meaning of the impression, the same way I did as I studied the beach ball. There would often be a few moments until the next impression presented itself. Now, I've found that Spirit will send it as fast as I can take it, which means I read in a flow state most often, and the words come out quickly. I often don't realize what I'm saying until I hear it just as the sitter does. I rarely remember anything that I've brought through when a reading is over.

There are a lot of misconceptions about how mediums communicate with spirits. Some people assume that we know any piece of information at any moment, or that we walk around seeing a handful of dead people surrounding each living person we see while we walk down the street. Neither of these things are true for any mediums that I've met.

There are many things I believe we're not meant to know. If it's true that we live multiple lives, I truly believe that we can't remember much from our previous lives because we're not supposed to. Perhaps approaching each lifetime with a beginner's mind is what allows us the most soul growth and evolution—which is why I believe we're here—so I'm leaning into that these days after so many conversations with those on the other side.

One of the things that so many people don't know is that mediums are interpreters when we speak to spirits. They deliver us single thoughts one at a time, and we still have to lean into the meaning behind whatever we might be seeing, hearing, feeling, knowing, smelling, or tasting with our clair senses. A beginner medium might have seen the beach ball and immediately assumed that their sitter liked beach balls or just bought one instead of realizing it was a symbol for an upcoming trip. Some mediums work with a lot of Spirit symbols. Spirit symbols are impressions that mean the same thing from one reading to another, and we'll discuss this topic in an upcoming chapter.

Only experience teaches you what things *tend* to mean after so many readings. When I feel a light squeeze on my heart, I know the spirit is telling me that they suffered cardiac arrest. If I feel two bumps on my heart instead, that means they suffered a heart attack. If I see a cigarette, this tends to mean that the passed spirit was a smoker. If I hear "dad" or "mom," which is pretty straightforward, I know I'm talking to a father or a mother. It sounds pretty simple, and it can be.

Other times it gets more complicated. When I see a rosary, this tends to mean that a passed spirit was Christian or of some religious denomination. But one time, I was bringing a father through who showed me a rosary, and I felt strongly that he wasn't a religious person at all. I shared this information with the sitter and described the look of the rosary. She knew exactly why he was showing me this wooden rosary. She told me a mentor had given it to her as a gift years ago, and at the time of her father's funeral, she and her mother felt like perhaps they should put something sacred in the casket with him. My sitter, his daughter, dug into her purse and tossed the rosary into his casket!

This is why I tell my students, and often remind myself, that it is so very important to never make assumptions during a reading. Even as an experienced medium, it can be easy to make an assumption or jump to interpret too quickly when you receive an impression. Your mind may get turned on if you're panicked and jump into thinking mode about the meaning behind what you're sensing. If I hadn't taken the time to study the beach ball without making assumptions, I easily could have gone down the wrong path and missed the crucial message that was coming through from my sitter's passed mother.

What I practice myself and encourage my students to do is to lean into the impressions and really experience them with my clair sense(s), giving the impression time to unfold. What do I mean by that? Remember that Spirit sends one impression after another. You may hear a sound, see an image, or feel a sensation in your body to start, but it may not be until the next impression from Spirit that you come to understand the meaning behind what you heard, saw, or felt. I didn't immediately know that the beach ball represented a trip to the Philippines or the deeper meaning of that trip to my sitter's mother. I had to focus on the impression and wait for more to follow while allowing my clair senses to begin to work in conjunction. We must be patient as mediums and stay with the trail of impressions so that we don't jump to interpret or make an assumption too quickly.

Here's another example. Let's say Spirit shows you an image of an apple. You immediately start making assumptions and jumping to interpret before taking the time to lean into that impression. You fall into the trap of asking your sitter assumptive questions, "Was your Mom a teacher?" Your sitter says no. "Did she live in New York City?" Your sitter says no again. If you were in my class, this is the point that I would jump in and say, "You're getting something legit from Spirit, but before putting the work of the medium on your sitter by asking them questions, lean into the impression and let it unfold."

You allow the image of the apple to return. You start to get the feeling that this sitter's mother liked apples, and a moment after that, you realize that it feels like she's trying to share a memory. You share this with your sitter and your sitter smiles, "Yes, she did, and I know the memory she's talking about." You lean in further, and the next thing that comes to mind is the image of an apple orchard. It turns out that this sitter and their family picked apples together each fall and then made homemade cider. This was a powerful memory for the sitter, and it brings tears to their eyes.

Can you see why it's so important to lean into each impression to let the next one follow? This is a medium's job, but if we panic, we turn our job into what looks like a bit of a guessing game. I call this putting your work on the sitter, which you want to avoid. Not to mention that it doesn't make us look that great as mediums because it sounds like we're just fishing, even if we really are getting legit impressions from Spirit.

You'll also come to realize that mediumship is about more than just speaking to Spirit. We as mediums are not only interpreters, but storytellers. Each time you sit down with someone, you carry the rather large responsibility of sharing the story of their passed loved one that intertwines with their currently unfolding story. Spirit is sharing their story through you. When you first begin as a medium, it may feel more like you're getting pieces of evidence here and there and only just managing to eke out a short and simple message that somewhat pulls all of the pieces together. As you progress, you'll notice how Spirit brilliantly does the work for you of putting all of the pieces together and creating a powerful story over the course of the reading you give. You may start to notice that the sequence in which they give evidence is significant and that one thing leads to another in quite an orderly fashion.

Earlier on in the same "beach ball" reading, my sitter's mother had described the friction she had had with her daughter and the way she and the sitter's father had parented differently. She spoke of her deep fear that her daughter would get into trouble and forget her heritage and where she came from. She also shared that she herself had never felt at home in the United States and had deeply mourned leaving her home country.

The order that she shared information throughout the reading was key. First, she set the stage for deeper understanding about why she had acted the way she had. She acknowledged the way she had parented strictly and how that had affected her daughter. This opened up her daughter for an ending of thanks that she could receive in a powerful and heartfelt way. To end the reading, this mother finally recognized the efforts her daughter was making that this mother's fear had stopped her from being able to see many times when she was alive.

Spirit knows how to communicate moving evidence and messages and often wants to deliver deeper meaning, understanding, or even an explanation to a sitter that they feel will bring them joy, peace, or the lifting of a burden.

As we jump into understanding each of the different clair senses, you'll notice that I list exercises you can practice to help you with your development. Every set of practices includes an exercise that requires you to give a reading while using only one of the clairs. I call this isolating the clair senses. I have found with myself and with my students that it's powerful and effective to incorporate this as a part of your development. While some clairs will feel more natural to you than others, think of it as helping you to strengthen all of your clair muscles so that you have more tools in your toolbox. I promise you that each spirit you encounter will speak to you differently though a combination of the clair senses. The more you can expand your toolbox and use all of the clair senses that are available to you to some degree, the less you'll get stumped and the more ways you'll have to receive a spiritual impression accurately. For example, if I was only skilled at using my clairvoyance and clairaudience, I would have still seen the beach ball and heard the words "vacation" and "Philippines." But I might not have been unable to convey the depth of the message behind this evidence if I wasn't also skilled at using my clairsentience, my ability to feel, and my claircognizance, my ability to know.

It's important to find joy in communicating with Spirit and to *not* take ourselves too seriously, even though mediumship is a sacred practice. This is why I call my mediumship development circles my "playgrounds" for my students. Spirit wants you to delight in your work, and they're not like judgy high-schoolers, so park your self-deprecation at the door unless you want your development to take a hell of a lot longer. Exercises aren't meant for you to ace. They're meant to challenge you and help you out of your comfort zone so that you can grow. I strongly suggest that you take this approach with the exercises in this book and in every learning environment that you encounter.

If I hadn't challenged myself with tough exercises to develop my mediumship, I wouldn't have gotten to the point where the message from my sitter's mother could flow out and greatly affect her in a positive way. She told me after the reading that she hadn't put the pieces together about how her mother's sadness in leaving her home country was connected to the fear that she felt about how her daughter might grow up. My sitter wrote this in my feedback survey the next day: "Sitting with Mel is so worth it. It's like hearing things you didn't know your soul and heart needed to hear. Highly recommend!" This is why learning the language of Spirit is so worth the work!

Ready to learn some Spirit speak?

Clairvoyance

Clairvoyance is of French origin and translates into "clear-seeing." It is the ability to see images through thought in your mind's eye. It is associated with the third eye chakra, which can be found just above the space between your eyebrows on your forehead.

Clairvoyance is one of the most common clairs used by beginning mediums. Think of how much we use our sight as living people. This makes clairvoyance one of the most accessible and easy to use clairs for most people. Most mediums see clairvoyantly by having an image flash in their mind or sometimes even play out like a very short movie reel, not unlike in a daydream. In fact, in dreams and daydreams, clairvoyance is extremely active. Have you ever had a dream or a daydream where you *didn't* see something, but only heard and felt things? Probably not, and if so, you're rare!

Students ask me constantly if it's normal that they don't always see images with lots of clarity. Perhaps the image is slightly blurry, fuzzy, or lacks as much detail as when they are seeing with their eyes.

This is normal. For any and all of the mediums I know, they often don't perceive spiritual impressions via *any* clair to be as clear when we're working subjectively as the senses we use as a living person.

When I first began as a medium, I identified spirits mainly through clairvoyance. While I use clairsentience now to identify the role of the spirit, I still additionally see spirits clairvoyantly, and rarely do I see any facial features. For me, they look more like a silhouette or a blurred-out image of a face, like in the TV show *Unsolved Mysteries.* The exception for seeing facial features and clothing is usually when a spirit wants to spotlight a feature about themselves that is very distinctive and will be easily recognizable to the sitter. I've asked Spirit to work with me this way because throughout the course of someone's lifetime, their appearance changes so much from hair length and color to weight, clothing style, etc., that I don't find this evidence to be the most powerful, generally speaking.

Once I gave a reading to a woman and brought through a close family friend who was like a grandmother to her. This grandmother figure showed me a large pizza as clearly as I've ever seen clairvoyantly. It looked kind of cartoon-like in my mind and just floated right in front of me. At first I had no idea the significance of the pizza. As I leaned into the spiritual impression, I heard "pizza party." As I continued to lean in, I saw a birthday party playing out. I related to my sitter that I felt this pizza was about a special birthday pizza party that had happened that both she and the passed spirit were at. While she said she didn't understand it being a birthday party, she validated that their family was Sicilian and that making pizzas was a huge family tradition. After the reading, she contacted me and told me that her mom reminded her that they *did* have a pizza party birthday celebration for her that this grandmother figure attended.

Clairvoyant Exercises

1) Studying faces (in person and in your mind's eye)

Ask a friend or family member if they'd be willing to help you with this exercise. For about three minutes, sit facing each other and study their features. Take in as much detail as you can. Look for aspects of their appearance that you might not always notice. Take more time if you need it to make sure that you're not rushing yourself.

After three minutes or so, close your eyes and see their face in your mind. Challenge yourself to notice as many details as you did when you were actually looking at them. Try to see with as much clarity as possible. You can make notes of the small details you are seeing in your mind's eye, then check if you were "seeing" them accurately clairvoyantly. You might be surprised by how much of a workout this can feel like. This exercise can help immensely with seeing more detail on the face of a spirit that you become aware of.

2) People watching

Our goal is always to expand your frame of reference, which is what Spirit uses to help communicate a message to a loved one through you. By closely observing more people more often, you'll expand your spiritual toolbox with more examples of how different humans look. Some of the best places to watch people are parks or shopping centers. Of course, you don't want to look like a creeper, but it seems normal enough to me to sit on a bench in either space and observe all of the people around you. Sit for fifteen to thirty minutes, and take in as many details about the people who pass by or are in your environment. You might notice their clothes, facial expressions, movements, hairstyles, etc. All of what you take in expands your frame of reference and gets banked in your spiritual toolbox!

3) Study nature and animals on a walk or a hike.

How often do you get out on a walk or hike in a natural area? How often when you're out on a hike or a walk are you truly present and taking in everything about your surroundings in great detail? There's a beautiful state park not far from my house with gorgeous hiking trails. On the path, we see squirrels, birds, deer, and sometimes the occasional snake. I've been lucky to avoid running into mountain lions so far! The trees on this trail are stunning, and fall is my favorite time to hike and watch the leaves turn color. Sometimes there is still water running down the mountains into small streams.

Find a nature walk or hike that you can go on. Put away your phone and turn off any music. Do your best to be present as you walk through and take in the beauty of nature in as much detail as you can. The more you notice and observe what you see, the more Spirit can rely on these images and this experience when necessary.

4) Clairvoyant memory game

Have you ever played the game Memory? I played it as a kid and play it with my daughter now. It's one of my favorites. I've got a clairvoyant memory game for you that's a bit different but just as fun. Place about ten to twelve items out on a table. Arrange them however you'd like, then take about three minutes to study the items. Notice details about them and where they are located in relation to each other on the table. Take in colors, shapes, height and width— whatever you can notice as you observe. After those three minutes, go into another room with a piece of paper and a pencil. Sketch out the items on the table as accurately as you can. Note every tiny detail that you can remember. Label colors as well. Draw the items in proportion to each other, and arrange them as you saw them laid out. Give yourself five to ten minutes to draw as much of what you saw as you can. Then come back into the room and see how you did! This is a great way to stretch your clairvoyant skills by using your mind's eye to remember what you saw.

5) Projecting images

Find a partner to do this exercise with. I like to choose a medium friend of mine for this one, since they already understand the concept of clairvoyance and communication through thought. Each of you will need a piece of paper and something to write with. Take turns thinking about a specific image in your mind and then intending to project it to your partner. For example, let's say that you bring the image of a red apple to mind and then intend to project that to your friend. They will focus and expand their awareness clairvoyantly to see if they can receive the same image that you've brought to mind. They'll take time to write down what they see before taking a turn themself so that you can see what you receive and write it down. Do this three times back and forth, then compare notes and see if either of you were able to accurately receive the images that were sent.

6) Clairvoyant symbols with Spirit

This is one of my all-time favorite exercises, and it's worked very well for me. Think about three pieces of evidence that you'd like to get during a reading more often and more accurately. I remember once writing down these three: divorce, suicide, and whether a person is living or passed. I sat down quietly and brought the first image to mind that I could think of for each piece of evidence. For divorce, it was a stack of papers that had a large stamp over the top that said "divorce," or divorce papers. For suicide, it was an image of a person pointing a finger at themselves in the chest area as if to say, "I made the decision myself." For a person who was living, I saw a simple stick figure face with a smile and open eyes. For a spirit who was passed, I saw the same stick figure face but with the eyes as Xs. In the next hour, I gave a reading, and Spirit used my divorce papers. It was accurate, too! I was *so* excited. I still use all of these symbols today, and they are accurate more than ninety-five percent of the time.

Once you have your three pieces of evidence, sit quietly for a few minutes just focusing on your breath. Then, in your mind's eye, think of the first piece of evidence and see what image comes to mind without too much effort. Do the same for all three pieces of evidence, and note them in a Spirit Shorthand Journal. Over the next month, review them quickly about three times a week. See if Spirit uses them in your readings!

7) Isolate the clair; isolate the evidence.

This is an exercise we do often in my mediumship development circle. Find someone who is willing to sit with you for a practice reading. Make sure that they are clear about the fact that you are just practicing and that you will be focusing on receiving all of your spiritual impressions clairvoyantly. This is what I call isolating a clair. Make sure they also understand that instead of giving them a full blown reading, you'll be focusing *only* on a specific shortlist of information. Once you do this, begin by quieting your mind and blending with Spirit. Then do your best to do what we call "anchoring the link," also known as identifying the spirit. This means that you'll do your best to identify someone who is recognizable to your sitter before proceeding on to these specific pieces of evidence that lend themselves to clairvoyance:

- See and describe their appearance before they passed. In particular, see their hands, and lean into what their hands indicate to you about how they spent their time when they were alive.
- See their home before they passed.
- See where they lived geographically near the end of their life.

- See a keepsake that belonged to them when they were alive that has been kept by the sitter or someone close to the spirit.
- *Bonus:* See an obscure piece of evidence or information that is special and specific but recognizable to the sitter that no one else would know.

As a disclaimer, these exercises can be quite challenging when you are just beginning and even when you've been practicing mediumship for some time! Please don't get down on yourself if you feel like you majorly bomb these practices, especially when you're first trying them. Over time, you will become more skilled if you put in the work.

Something else to keep in mind is that exercises to strengthen our clair muscles can feel much more challenging than giving an actual reading, whether intuitively or mediumistically. Give it your all with each exercise, and just have fun. Remember that any time you practice, you are building your ability to use the language of Spirit and to expand your toolbox!

Clairaudience

Clairaudience translates into "clear-hearing." It is the ability to hear sounds through thought in your mind. It is associated with the throat chakra.

One thing I love about clairaudience is that it is one of the clearest clairs. This is because when you hear a word or a combination of a few words, there often isn't as much interpretation required as there might be for an image or feeling. That being said, clairaudience isn't always hearing words; it can be hearing any kind of sound. If you hear the sound of a screeching car, that might tell you that the spirit passed in a car accident. Maybe if you hear the sound of birds, the spirit is trying to tell you that they send signs to their loved one via birds, or perhaps they are describing sounds that they heard outside their home before passing.

Many people mistake their own thoughts and mind chatter for clairaudience. While having your own thoughts and mind chatter is definitely a reality, a lot of times when ideas suddenly drop into our head and we hear them as thoughts, we are actually receiving information clairaudiently.

If you were to say to yourself in your mind, "Hi me, I love you," then you would experience what it's like to hear clairaudiently. Yup, it's not more complicated than that—except that instead of saying things to yourself in your mind, these sounds just drop in and are not of you. If you have a strong propensity toward clairaudience, you probably hear songs play over and over in your mind. You may also be very sensitive to sounds, especially loud noises. Keep in mind that clairaudient impressions usually aren't as clear as when you hear a living person, noise, or yourself talking out loud. Also, don't expect long sentences. You're more likely to get a word, a short phrase, or a sound.

When I first began discovering my mediumistic skills, clairaudience was one of my more dominant clairs, and it's still one that I use frequently when I communicate with Spirit. I remember a time when my family was visiting and staying with us for Christmas. We had all gone out for dinner. Afterward, I went home, but my sister and my mom stayed out later and had drinks with more family members. I was asleep around midnight when I was nearly thrown out of bed and heard clairaudiently, "Your sister needs help. She can't get home."

I didn't get the sense that she was in danger, but I felt I had to call my sister. When she picked up the phone, she said, "You're still awake? We're fine. We're just having a hard time getting home because there aren't any cabs." Then she said quickly that a car was finally pulling up and she had to go. I thought it was strange that I'd been woken up just for that, so I went back to bed. As soon as I laid my head down I heard clairaudiently, "Put your phone beside your pillow." We have a rule in our house that electronics are not allowed in bedrooms, especially phones, but I could tell that I wouldn't be getting sleep unless I followed these instructions. I got my phone, put it near my pillow and laid down. Within thirty seconds it was ringing, and my sister was calling. "Sorry Mel, but we're at the gate to your neighborhood, and I don't know the code!" Rob and I never stay out late enough to need the code, so I'd completely forgotten that she'd need it.

Clairaudience is how I hear names during readings. I also tend to hear the name of illnesses and medical conditions while I feel sensations throughout my body. There was a time I was giving a reading for a woman who had lost her mother. I suddenly felt cold liquid running through my veins. It was a pretty intense feeling, and then I heard clairaudiently, "Dialysis." Sure enough, her mother had had dialysis when she was ill before passing. When I identify the role a spirit played to my sitter, I usually get a sense for who it might be, but then I often hear, "mother," "dad," etc.

Clairaudient Exercises

1) Listen to music like this.

Choose a song to listen to. I highly recommend classical music due to the many different instruments you can pick from for this exercise, but any song will do. As you listen to the song, choose *only* one instrument to isolate and listen to. I often put my focus around my temple area, where our clairaudient sensors stem from, and imagine my awareness expanding. I listen to hear as much detail as possible from this instrument and to hear it as clearly as I possibly can. I think of it as listening beyond what we hear with our ears in everyday life. I enjoy this exercise because music is one of the things I love most. It's a challenging exercise, and it's fun!

2) Listen for sounds.

This is an exercise to do when it is quiet, so if your house is a chaotic or noisy environment at the moment, you'll need to escape to somewhere more peaceful. Sit down in a comfortable position, and put your focus on your temple area, where your clairaudience stems from. Intend to expand your awareness to be able to hear beyond the normal everyday sounds that we hear with our ears. Now listen for those sounds that you're unlikely to notice as you go about your day. Perhaps you can hear a creak down the hall, a quiet birdsong outside the window that is further away, or the rhythm of the dryer on the other side of the house. Focus on each of these sounds, and hear them as clearly as you can and with as much detail as possible.

3) Take in the sounds of nature.

This exercise is all about being present with the sounds of nature. Take a walk or hike in nature, and listen intently to the sounds that you hear. It's about focusing your mind and attention on every little rustle and wisp of breeze that you encounter. When I go hiking with my family, I don't usually notice the sound of the crunch under my hiking boots as I step over fall leaves and pebbles on the path. I most definitely don't hear the sound of a calm breeze if we take my three year old along with us. Remember that every sound you register is added to your frame of reference, and this expands your toolbox that Spirit uses when they communicate with you. This is another one of my favorite exercises, since hiking is a beloved activity of mine.

4) Pay attention to voices.

A strong piece of evidence can be describing the distinct voice of a passed loved one. My grandfather had a voice that was unique and reminded me somewhat of Jimmy Stewart. It was also a bit gravely, and he wheezed when he laughed as he got older. You can practice this exercise in a couple of different ways. It can be powerful to imagine the sound of someone's voice. I like to imagine the voice of someone I know well, like my daughter, my husband, or my parents. I try to hear their voice as clearly and with as much detail as if they were really there speaking to me. Sometimes I'll imagine the phrases they say most often, and it'll make me laugh or smile or make my heart swell.

Another way you can practice this exercise is by paying attention to the sounds of different voices if you're having dinner with friends at a gathering or get together, or just at home with family. It's helpful to notice the difference between them and details like their tone, cadence, and pitch.

5) Isolate the clair; isolate the evidence.

This is an exercise we do often in my mediumship development circle. Find someone who is willing to sit with you for a practice reading. Make sure that they are clear about the fact that you are just practicing and that you will be focusing on receiving all of your spiritual impressions clairaudiently. This is what I call isolating a clair. Make sure they also understand that instead of giving them a full blown reading, you will be focusing *only* on a specific shortlist of information. Once you do this, begin by quieting your mind and blending with Spirit. Then do your best to do what we call anchoring the link, also known as identifying the spirit. That means that you'll do your best to identify someone who is recognizable to your sitter before proceeding on to these specific pieces of evidence that lend themselves to clairaudience:

- Hear and describe the sound of their voice.
- Hear sounds in and around their home before they passed.
- Hear the genre or type of music they listened to. For an extra challenge, see if you can hear their favorite song.
- Hear how they passed.
- Hear their name.
- *Bonus:* Hear a final conversation that was had before passing or an important conversation that was exchanged at some point with the sitter.

Clairsentience

Clairsentience translates into "clear-feeling." It is the ability to feel through thought in your mind. It is associated with the heart chakra and the solar plexus chakra.

I'll admit right away that clairsentience is one of my absolute favorite clairs, and although I didn't consider it my most dominant clair when I began, it has become a tool that I use religiously when speaking to Spirit. Why do I love clairsentience so much? Think about it like this: Humans are feeling creatures who listen to music, tell stories, watch movies, fall in love, make love, desire relationships, and more because of how they make us feel. While not all feelings are pleasant, we *live* to feel. If we aren't feeling much, then it's likely we're not really living.

When someone visits a medium, what they want more than anything is to feel as if they are getting time with their passed loved one again. While it may be sexy to get evidence such as their name, age, where they lived geographically, etc., what really moves and heals a sitter, in my experience, is feeling the character and personality of their loved one come through; of getting a message from them that hits the spot; and of feeling that they are truly present because of how well the relationships, mannerisms, and tendencies of their loved one is brought through.

Clairsentience is such a powerful tool in this way. I like to ask Spirit to come quite close when I work so I can really feel how they were, who they were, and their feelings about life and toward my sitter. I love to feel them so strongly that I can let words pour out of me that they've been eager and waiting to say to their loved one since they passed.

Clairsentience can be felt in several different ways. You might feel emotions. Perhaps your heart feels full, and this signals the love a passed spirit has for the sitter. Maybe you feel remorse and regret, indicating that the spirit has apologies to make. Perhaps you feel a bit like laughing and realize that this spirit had a sense of humor and was a funny person who liked to tease and joke around.

Sometimes clairsentience is getting a feeling about the role that they played. While it's difficult to describe what a mother, father, sister, brother, aunt, uncle, daughter, or grandparent *feels like*, this is something that mediums can clairsentiently sense about a spirit.

Clairsentience can also include feeling textures. Perhaps you're feeling satin sheets on a bed or a soft towel because that's the way the laundry always felt at your grandfather's house. Maybe you're feeling a scruffy beard on your face or hand that is exactly what your sitter's dad's face felt like. You may also feel sensations in different parts of your body that indicate something about the way that they moved or an illness they suffered from that caused their passing.

I gave a reading for a woman whose husband had passed. I started to feel like I had an intense headache that was on the top of my head and then traveled down the back of my head as well. I mentioned this to her, and she nodded. A moment later, I heard "brain tumor," and that was indeed how he had passed. Often when a Spirit is immobile at the end of their life and bedridden, I feel stiff. When they have trouble speaking or communicating, my words are jumbled or my throat is tight. When my words became jumbled in this same reading with the spirit who had suffered a brain tumor, that let me know that he was unable to communicate to his wife before he died, and she confirmed this as well.

Clairsentient Exercises

1) Relive a memory.

Reliving a memory is a great way to strongly activate clairsentience. I suggest picking a memory that stands out as a very important event in your life and that includes at least one other person. Memories are a powerful tool because you often get the chance to feel in many different ways. For example, as you replay the memory in your mind, you might start with revisiting the time of year that it took place and allowing yourself to feel the weather. You could have been cold and shivering, hot and sweaty, feeling the fall breeze, etc. You can spend time feeling into who you were as a person at that time, your feelings toward anyone else who was there, and what your relationship with them was like. Perhaps you can feel physical sensations in your body, as well, to remind you of movements or even an illness or cause of passing if it was a time when you lost a loved one. Whatever this memory presents in terms of feeling, give yourself permission to expand your clairsentient awareness. Truly open yourself up to feeling in as many different ways as possible and with as much clarity and detail as possible.

2) Feel into the role of the spirit (to the sitter).

This exercise can really help you take your mediumship to the next level in terms of anchoring the link, also known as identifying the role of the spirit to the sitter. Was the spirit the sitter's mother, father, sister, brother, child, grandparent, friend, etc.? Regardless of how you run your readings, all of the evidence that you bring will be much more powerful in terms of healing if your sitter quickly understands what spirit is presently being brought through by you. At the beginning of their journeys, many mediums find this to be challenging. They may be able to identify the gender, age range, character, and personality of a passed spirit, but to know for sure what their exact role was can be trickier. With this exercise, it may be helpful to sit in the power briefly before beginning and setting the intention that Spirit will assist you. Then, as you feel strongly blended with Spirit, ask them to show you how it feels clairsentiently when a mother draws near. Continue on to other family members, like a friend who isn't a family relation, maybe a co-worker, and so on. You can cycle through as many roles as you like, but I like to keep it to about four or five roles and really take my time feeling into each role. Perhaps you'll be pleasantly surprised, and Spirit will use it in an upcoming reading!

3) Pay attention to the weather and outdoor surroundings.

This is a fun one and not unlike the outdoor walks and hikes. With this exercise, pay attention to the weather and your outdoor surroundings. It's a plus if you live somewhere that experiences all four seasons. We live by three lakes, and when I go paddle boarding with my family, we often sit in silence and enjoy the stillness of the lake, the herons that fly over the it, and the cool breeze that comes off the water. In the winter, I know both the physical sensations and the emotional excitement that comes with the first snow of the season and the upcoming anticipation of the holidays. I can recall time I spent in Bali when it was nearly ninety percent humidity and the temperature was in the eighties or nineties. My body was always sweaty, and I felt as if I was perpetually living in a sauna. I also recall the sound of the ocean waves and the feel of sand under my feet when I walked on the beach. With this exercise, when you are outside, cut out all distractions like cell phones, and be present with how the elements feel to you on all levels.

4) Feel the cause of passing.

To be able to understand how a spirit passed is a powerful piece of evidence. It can play a big role in bringing deep healing, and it can validate to your sitter that their loved one is truly present. This can also be a challenging piece of evidence for many mediums, especially at the beginning of their journeys. Mediums who have extensive knowledge of the body and illnesses, like EMTs, doctors, surgeons, nurses, etc., are often quite skilled in this area of evidence. While it sounds morbid, I like to start by researching the top ten causes of death. I make a list of them, and I include whatever cause of passing is most common in my readings. I take a brief amount of time to sit in the power, blend with Spirit, and set the intention that they assist me. I then ask Spirit to show me what different causes of passing feel like to me clairsentiently. I limit myself to experiencing three or four causes of passing so that I can take my time to explore each one clearly and in detail. I strongly set the intention that these feelings get added to my spiritual toolbox and that Spirit use them during my readings when applicable. A quick note that when you clairsentiently "feel" the cause of passing, it is often quite subtle instead of being extremely unpleasant. If for any reason the sensations are strong and unpleasant, you can tell Spirit to back off a bit, and they will.

5) Photo readings

While you can use photos to practice strengthening any one of your clair senses, I like to use photo readings especially for clairsentient development. There are a couple of ways to go about this. Many teach to look at the picture of the passed person and focus on their eyes, then to focus on the feelings that this person was feeling at the time the picture was taken. This can work well. Another tactic I use is to study the person in the picture, but then let it go from my mind and intend for the spirit to draw close, shifting all of my attention away from the photo and toward the feeling of the spirit that I'm now linking to.

My reason for using this second approach is that looking at a picture will often turn on your thinking mind. It takes us less than a few seconds to make all kinds of unconscious assumptions about a person based on their appearance. Instead, we want our thinking mind off and our blend with the spirit to lead us to accurate spiritual impressions. Try both ways, and see what works best for you. I'll discuss photo readings more in an upcoming chapter, but for this exercise, focus on feeling clairsentiently, and see if you can bring through this evidence:

- Gender
- Age range when they passed *(infant, young child, teenager, young adult, middle-aged, above middle aged, older)*
- Role they played to the sitter *(mother, father, sister, brother, grandmother, grandfather, son, daughter, extended family, friend)*
- Personality and character
- Cause of passing

6) Isolate the clair; isolate the evidence.

This is an exercise we do often in my mediumship development circle. Find someone who is willing to sit with you for a practice reading. Make sure that they are clear about the fact that you are just practicing and that you will be focusing on receiving all of your spiritual impressions clairsentiently. This is what I call isolating a clair. Make sure they also understand that instead of giving them a full blown reading, that you will be focusing *only* on a specific shortlist of information. Once you do this, begin by quieting your mind and blending with Spirit. Then do your best to do what we call "anchoring the link," also known as identifying the spirit. That means that you'll do your best to identify someone who is recognizable to your sitter before proceeding on to these specific pieces of evidence, that you saw in the previous section, that lend themselves to clairsentience:

- Gender
- Age range when they passed, *(infant, young child, teenager, young adult, middle-aged, above middle aged, older)*
- Role they played to the sitter *(mother, father, sister, brother, grandmother, grandfather, son, daughter, extended family, friend)*
- Personality and character
- Cause of passing

Claircognizance

Claircognizance translates into "clear-knowing." It is the ability to access your true inner knowing. It is associated with the crown chakra.

Claircognizance can be tricky to recognize initially because it doesn't require interpretation like other clairs. It doesn't come with any physical sensations, pictures, or sounds. When you receive a claircognizant spiritual impression, it simply pops into your mind, and you just *know*. When mediums start receiving impressions claircognizantly, they may wonder if they're making the information up because it isn't identifiable in terms of which clair sense it's coming through except that it's that sudden understanding about something that you didn't have a moment ago. You might suddenly know how someone passed; what a spirit wants to say; and just about anything about a spirit, location, or something that took place. Perhaps you've called it a "sudden download" that you get.

If clairsentience is one of my favorite clairs, claircognizance is the other that I absolutely adore—although I love them all! Why do I love claircognizance so much? For me, claircognizance paired with clairsentience is one of the most powerful ways to deliver messages with incredible depth and details in a flow state that is so very healing for your sitter. A flow state is when evidence and messages are coming through in a way that feels more like it's a stream of consciousness, although it makes perfect sense and is detailed and accurate.

Claircognizance is something I didn't realize that I'd been using my entire life. Throughout my life, I have felt tremendous clarity. It doesn't seem to matter the decision that I face; there have been very few times when I've felt that I don't quickly know precisely what I want or where I'd like to go with my life in just about every aspect. I'm quick to make decisions, and I can't think of many instances where I'd do things differently, even if they were really stupid decisions. To me, the path almost always feels clear, and the decision will either turn out well, or I'll learn a valuable lesson. Now, it's important to share that even so, I *didn't* consider it one of my best tools when I first began my work as a medium. While I have always been able to use claircognizance for myself, I wasn't initially able to use it mediumistically. That came with time.

Now, when I give readings, as the energy builds and the reading progresses, I often feel myself start to look directly at my sitter, sometimes shifting into first person, and just letting the words roll off my tongue about all the spirit has to say. I can't tell you how I know what they want to say. I just know, and I only understand it once it comes out of my mouth. In a way, I'm hearing it just as the sitter is. There are other moments when I get singular pieces of information that suddenly drop into my mind in a claircognizant way, too, but my favorite is when I access what I call the "flow state." Truly, it is an amazing clair that you've likely used before and that, when developed and honed, can become one of your most powerful tools.

Claircognizant Exercises

1) What will happen next list

This exercise is a whole lot of fun and a great way to strengthen your claircognizance. I like to make a list called "What Will Happen Next" and see how often I get it right. Here is a short list of good What Will Happen Next ideas:

- Who will text me next?
- Who will call me next?
- What kind of car will drive by next?
- Who will walk into this coffee shop next?
- What exact time will I drop my daughter off at preschool this morning?
- Who will I walk by in the grocery store next?

All I do is ask myself the question once, and then I often get a quick flash of an answer. There isn't time to think, and I notice the way it just drops into my mind. Not every question I ask feels easily received, but some do! The one I receive accurately almost any time I ask myself is the exact time that something will happen. If I ask exactly what time we'll leave the house in the morning and arrive at preschool, I often see that exact time on my phone.

I asked what car we would see next one day and quickly got the download that it was a blue Tesla. Sure enough, we pulled onto the main road, and a blue Tesla drove right by us. To be honest, I was in disbelief!

The first time I was introduced to this exercise, I practiced it at a coffee shop where I was working for the day. I asked who would walk into the coffee shop next. I got an image of a man with white trainers, a briefcase, glasses, and a baseball hat with bushy, curly gray hair spilling out from under the hat. The color of the hair had me assume that this was an older man. He was not the very next man that came into the coffee shop, but the third. I saw the shoes, briefcase, glasses, hat and hair, but the hair was blond, and he was a young man. Still, I was amazed at how powerful claircognizance can be!

Make your list, and see how often you're right! Pay close attention to how it comes to you as a quick flash and drops into your mind without any thought. You'll get better as you practice.

2) Automatic writing

Automatic writing is a great practice to help you develop your claircognizance because you are intending to turn your brain off and just let the words flow. I like to use a computer instead of writing in a notebook because I can type much faster than I write, and often the information will drop in quickly. I also like the exercise of automatic writing because I believe it's a great way to get better at delivering a powerful message during a mediumistic reading. To begin an automatic writing session, it's nice to sit in the power for a brief couple of minutes and feel that strong blend with Spirit, although you don't have to start this way. There's the option of just starting to write and seeing what comes.

I watched a documentary that featured a parent who felt a strong pull to journal after his son died and channeled messages directly from his son. This is a prime example of what's possible with automatic writing.

When I practice, and when I teach automatic writing, I set an intention about who I want to connect with and what I'd like an answer to. It might be your Higher Self, Spirit, Source, Universe, or whatever word works best for you. For a question, I like to ask, "What do I need to know today?"

Put on a timer for ten to twenty minutes when you're just starting out. As you begin writing, leave all judgment and thought aside. Simply write what comes to you without thinking. Avoid rereading or reviewing any of your writing until you're finished. If you begin by writing gibberish, that's great! It's a good sign that your brain is off and you're surrendering to the process. One of my favorite clues that I'm truly connected and channeling information is that I'll find myself using words I don't often use or that I don't even know the definitions of. When I look them up after and find that they make sense and are used within the context properly, I know I was connected.

Have fun—you might just blow your mind with what comes through! If you find this exercise challenging, just keep practicing, and you'll find it easier to connect over time.

3) Stream-of-consciousness mediumistic message

This exercise is not completely unlike the practice of automatic writing, but it's more like automatic speaking. It's a great way to practice isolating claircognizance. Find someone who is willing to sit with you for a practice reading. Make sure that they are clear about the fact that you are just practicing and that you will be focusing on connecting to a recognizable passed loved one and then going directly into a message that is delivered claircognizantly. Make sure they also understand that instead of giving them a full-blown reading with evidence preceding the message, you will be focusing *only* on the message and attempting to get into a flow state by leaning into what feels like your stream of consciousness. It's also good to let them know that just as in automatic writing, with this technique of delivering a message, it may initially sound like gibberish.

Once you do this, begin by quieting your mind and blending with Spirit. Then do your best to anchor the link, also known as identifying the spirit. That means that you'll do your best to identify someone who is recognizable to your sitter before proceeding on to the message. You will bring through evidence only to help identify the spirit as you would in a normal reading. Once you identify the spirit, ask them to come quite close to you, and imagine that they are so close that it's as if you're looking at your sitter through their eyes. Blend strongly with this spirit and without thinking, let their words flow out of you, giving a message from this spirit to your sitter. Do not have the sitter respond while you work. Instead, get feedback from them afterward, asking them if the message made sense to them and if it is something their passed loved one would say.

This exercise takes a lot of bravery, courage, and trust on your part. Preparing your sitter well and getting a sitter who you can be comfortable with is extremely helpful so that you can surrender to the process!

Clairalience and Clairgustance

Clairalience translates into "clear-smelling." It's the ability to sense smells through thought in your mind. Clairgustance translates into "clear-tasting." It's the ability to sense tastes through thought in your mind.

It's easy to underestimate just how powerful clairalient and clairgustant spiritual impressions can be! We focus on seeing, hearing, and feeling so often, but a smell we associate with a passed loved one or the taste of a food we enjoyed with them or that they used to bake, for example, can bring back powerful memories and be a highly cathartic experience for our sitters.

Many beginning mediums think that they should be objectively tasting or smelling when it comes to clairalience and clairgustance, but remember that most of us work subjectively, so when you say you smell or taste something, it's most common to experience it through thought. That means that you're tasting the idea of chocolate cake, or smelling the idea of cigarette smoke. For example, imagine walking down the street and starting to get a whiff of a bakery nearby. You can smell bread and sweet pastries. As you turn the corner, you come upon the door to the bakery and enter it. The sweet bready smell hits you, and it's sublime! You see donuts and spot your absolute favorite, a chocolate covered donut with chantilly cream. You wait in line with excitement and anticipation, your mouth watering and already tasting the delicious donut. When it's your turn, you order a hot coffee and the donut. You sit down and take a sip of the coffee, savoring the warm liquid inside your mouth and slowly swallowing it. Now you pick up the donut and bring it to your mouth, but before you even take your first bite, you breathe in the delectable aroma of chocolate, cream, and sweet dough.

I think you get the picture, right? Just taking yourself through that experience in your mind is what it feels like when you receive clairalient and clairgustant impressions. Of course, these kinds of impressions aren't limited to food at all. You might smell or taste something rather unpleasant, like the metallic smell and taste of blood. Perhaps you smell the scent of burnt rubber and smoke if a spirit is communicating to you a car accident. Maybe you smell flowers from someone who loved to garden or cigarette smoke from a spirit who smoked when they were alive.

While many mediums do receive these smells subjectively, as I shared, there may be moments when you receive a sign from a passed loved one and smell or taste objectively. I remember walking down my hallway and objectively smelling cigarette smoke. I promise you there is no way in hell that would be in our house, but it was. I instantly knew it was my paternal grandmother, who smoked like a chimney when she was alive.

There was another time that I was cooking in the kitchen, a beloved pastime of my maternal grandmother. I caught a strong whiff of the lotion she used to wear that you'd get a hit of every time you went into her bathroom. It was distinct, and you always knew Grandma Ann was nearby when you smelled it. I knew she was with me at that moment as I was making dinner, giving me props for my skills in the kitchen.

I was giving a group reading once in my home and brought through the beloved grandparents of a woman. Among the many pieces of evidence that I brought through were warm chocolate chip cookies, both the taste and smell. I knew that my sitter had played outside in her grandparent's yard as a child with her cousins, and when they all piled in the house afterward, the smell of chocolate chip cookies would hit them. They were delicious, and they would always be served warm. She burst into tears and confirmed this to be true.

Clairalient and Clairgustant Exercises

1) Red velvet cake with coffee or tea.

Clairgustant and clairalient exercises can be a lot of fun, but just be prepared that this one might get you craving a special treat! If you're not a red velvet cake fan, feel free to change the dessert in this exercise to something of your choice. The same goes for the beverage that accompanies it. Focus first on your breath, and get yourself into a slight meditative state. Imagine yourself entering the home of a friend who you're going to have dessert and a warm drink with. When you open the door to their home, the smell of the cake hits you, as does the hot coffee that is just brewing. Take yourself through tasting and smelling every detail of the dessert and hot drink with as much clarity as possible. You might be surprised how fast time flies when you take yourself through this experience. Give yourself time to enjoy it, slowly savoring each bite and sip.

2) Eat, then imagine.

A good way to develop your clairalience and clairgustance is to be incredibly present with smells and tastes. Savoring the smell of things and the tastes of food and drink is so very helpful in expanding your frame of reference and spiritual toolbox. Take your time with your foods and the things you drink, enjoying them with every sip and bite.

In this exercise, pick a food of your choice. I like to use dark chocolate or an apple. Sit and eat the food of your choice, being so very present with every bite and paying close attention to the details of the experience. When you've finished the food, see how closely you can relive the experience in your imagination, bringing forth both the taste and the smell of the food with as much detail and clarity as you possibly can.

3) Ask Spirit for smells and tastes.

Before you begin this exercise, it can be helpful to sit in the power for a couple of minutes and feel that strong blend with Spirit. I set the intention for Spirit to assist me in developing my clairalience and clairgustance as I ask them to bring me subjective smells and tastes that I can use as symbols. For example, I might ask Spirit to show me the smell of a smoker if a spirit smoked when they were alive. I may ask them to let me know when someone was an avid baker by bringing me the taste of a baked good. Here is a short list of smells and tastes that you can have Spirit help you to experience that can serve as symbols to help you understand the information that a spirit is bringing through:

- Taste or smell cigarette smoke when a spirit was a smoker.
- Smell burnt rubber or gasoline when a spirit experienced a car accident.
- Smell smoke when a spirit is communicating to you about a fire.
- Taste or smell baked goods when a spirit enjoyed baked treats or was a baker.
- Taste or smell savory foods when a spirit was a good cook.
- Taste alcohol when a spirit enjoyed a drink or suffered from alcoholism.
- Smell perfume when a spirit wore certain scents.

To try out my Mediumship Visualization Exercise, Clear Tasting and Smelling, use this QR code:

4) Isolate the clair; isolate the evidence.

This is an exercise we do often in my mediumship development circle. Find someone who is willing to sit with you for a practice reading. Make sure that they are clear about the fact that you are just practicing and that you will be focusing on receiving all of your spiritual impressions clairaliently and clairgustantly. This is what I call isolating a clair. Make sure they also understand that instead of giving them a full-blown reading, you will be focusing *only* on a specific shortlist of information. Once you do this, begin by quieting your mind and blending with Spirit. Then do your best to anchor the link. That means that you'll do your best to identify someone who is recognizable to your sitter before proceeding on to these specific pieces of evidence that lend themselves to clairalience and clairgustance:

- Smells associated with this passed loved one
- Favorite foods
- Favorite beverages
- Disliked foods
- Disliked beverages
- Any details about their cause of passing
- Did they smoke?

- Did they wear perfume?

Bringing Through Powerful Evidence and Working with Symbols

Keeping a Spirit Shorthand Journal

You remember that mediums are interpreters, right? You also know by now that spiritual impressions come in quick flashes and are just one single thought at a time. They can come via any of the clair senses, and often there is still the need to understand the meaning behind the thought. This is one of the tricky aspects of mediumship that can lead us to getting an impression that is absolutely legit but interpreting it incorrectly or describing it in a way that our sitter can't understand and then hearing "no." If you continue to practice and put in the work, you'll discover more about how your mediumship works and become more efficient. Efficiency really is key in mediumship because our sitters are eager to hear what their loved ones have to say. A reading is never as enjoyable for a sitter when a medium stumbles over their interpretation or takes longer than they'd like to understand what the spirit is trying to communicate. Wouldn't it be nice if every time we sensed a particular spiritual impression, it always meant the same thing from reading to reading?

Good news, that is what a symbol is in mediumship; it's a spiritual impression via any one of the clairs that holds the same meaning from reading to reading. I like to call it Spirit Shorthand.

When symbols come to mind, many mediums think of them as being only, or dominantly, clairvoyant, but many of the symbols I use are clairaudient, clairsentient, or clairalient as well. Others have symbols that are clairgustant, too, with the exception of claircognizance because it's knowing something suddenly and in the moment.

A lot of mediums also find symbols to be super sexy and are constantly wanting to build up their Spirit Shorthand Journal. While I am a lover of symbols and have found them to be extremely useful, keep in mind that not all mediums use them. I have a dear friend who is a high-quality medium, and symbols just don't come easily to her, but she still gives great readings. There are many ways to communicate with Spirit, so if symbols don't come easily or much at all, don't sweat it. That being said, because of the positive experience I and many of my students have had working with symbols, I suggest that you give it a try because of its potential effect of making your mediumship more efficient.

Maybe you're wondering how symbols are created in your practice? Sometimes you might discover a symbol that a spirit gives you *during* a reading. I remember bringing through a father for a mother and a daughter. I was asking the spirit how he had passed, and I quickly felt two quick pulses on my heart. It was incredibly subtle. As I usually do when an impression is new or very subtle, I decided to double check my evidence by asking the spirit to give me the impression again if that indeed was what he was communicating to me. I got the two pulses on my heart another time and then claircognizantly understood that these two pulses meant heart attack. The family members confirmed that this was how he had passed. Over the course of more readings, this clairsentient spiritual impression of two pulses on my heart showed itself to be a symbol for heart attack, while a light squeeze on my heart indicated cardiac arrest. With experience, you will learn over time what impressions are symbols for you. However, I will usually get the sense that what I'm receiving as an impression isn't for literal interpretation and that it is likely a symbol without having to have multiple readings that use that spiritual impression the same way to confirm it's a symbol. For example, let's say I'm seeing an apple during a reading and it doesn't seem like it means the spirit is literally handing the sitter an apple. As I lean into that impression of the apple, I then get the clairsentient and clairvoyant impressions that this apple is actually a symbol for living in New York City because I see the city's skyline in my mind and feel like I'm in a big city. To be able to decipher whether an impression is a symbol or not, I teach my students what I call *"resonance"* and *"dissonance."* We can all feel the inner resonance within us when we take in information that feels like truth. Or, we can feel the inner dissonance within us when we take in information that does not feel aligned with the truth or isn't a match. Here's what it might look like to use this technique during a reading: Let's say you get a clairvoyant image of a hot air balloon, as I did during a reading once. As you study this hot air balloon, it may not initially be clear whether this means your sitter has taken a ride in a hot air balloon or whether the hot air balloon is symbolic. In your mind, you ask Spirit, "Are you telling me that my sitter rode in a hot air balloon?" You feel dissonance. You then ask Spirit, "Is this hot air balloon a symbol?" Not only do you feel resonance, but more spiritual impressions follow.

Your sitter is now in the hot air balloon in the image you see, and she's floating up above a generation of her family members. You realize that this is symbolic for her recent understanding and new perspective of behaviors in the family that were carried on by many of the women in the family. Her new perspective is letting her transcend some of those old behaviors that she still sees playing out in family dynamics. This is exactly what happened for me during a reading, and my client quickly confirmed that she had just recently been discussing this in therapy. She felt that the perspective shift had freed her in many ways and was deeply moved and healed by the acknowledgement and validation that came from the spirit of her maternal grandmother.

You might be wondering if you can ask Spirit to use a symbol of your choice. Absolutely! At least half of the symbols that I use consistently are symbols that I shared with Spirit and then asked them to use in my readings. It's easy to do, and it doesn't take a long ritual or anything of the sort to implement this practice. Whenever I reflect on the information that I'd like to get more easily and efficiently during a reading, I bring a symbol to mind and hold it there for Spirit to sense. I strongly intend and ask that they use it during my readings. When I do this, I generally make a list of three new symbols a week over a month's time that I'd love to add to my Spirit Shorthand Journal. I will review those three new symbols about three times a week for the next month to securely add them to my frame of reference and spiritual toolbox. I'm not constantly adding new symbols to my journal each week these days, but I've gone through seasons where I worked more diligently on my Spirit Shorthand.

Something you should know right from the beginning is that Spirit will likely *not* use every symbol that you give them, and even a symbol that they've given you may only be used a single time. I'd guess that Spirit has used about forty to fifty percent of the symbols that I've created—and some much more often than others.

Another thing to keep in mind with your symbols is the gentle reminder that your mediumship will never stay the same. You may remember that I was a symbol girl early on in my development. Now I only use a fraction of those symbols. I'd say I have less than a dozen that are steadfast. I have a divorce symbol, a suicide symbol, a dead or alive symbol, etc., and often the rest comes to me in other ways that are just as efficient or even more so. Because I work clairsentiently and claircognizantly much more than I used to, it turns out I have less need for symbols. No matter how my mediumship changes, it seems that Spirit really only wants to assist you in progressing your skills.

What Evidence to Ask For

Evidence is what we call information about a spirit that a medium brings through during a reading, specifically information that can be validated. For example, the gender of the spirit, the cause of passing, whether they had pets, etc. Information that is not evidential would be things the medium is communicating from the spirit that cannot be validated, such as what the spirit's experience was on the other side after passing, whether the spirit sent a sitter's current partner to them after passing, what the spirit is up to on the other side, etc.

What evidence should you be focusing on when you work mediumistically? It's a great question. Sitters do come to us with expectations and hopes around who will come through and what they might say, no matter how much we caution them to be open during the experience. The other question that goes hand in hand with what evidence to focus on is whether you should be asking Spirit questions as you work or if they will just start communicating to you what they want to share.

Spirit works off of our frames of reference. That means that whatever is most easily accessible within our mind to get clear communication across will be used by Spirit and can sometimes dictate what evidence is shared or how it's brought through.

I like to remind my students that there is no one right way to communicate with Spirit. What matters is that we communicate with as much accuracy as possible and through our work are creating an experience for our sitters that brings them peace, healing, and whatever it is Spirit knows they need most. Because each medium works in such a unique fashion, you might be the kind of medium that feels you can "interview" the spirit and ask questions during a reading to bring through evidence and a message. I took a course once that focused on "interviewing the spirit." I found that way of working really helpful when I practiced photo readings, but when giving readings to live sitters, interviewing the spirit has never worked well for me.

When Spirit works with me, they know what they want to share and say to their passed loved one. Spiritual impressions come to me one after another about as quickly as I can handle them. I often read in a flow state, which means that I don't really have time to ask questions. As I shared earlier, Communication and the Clairs, Spirit is highly intelligent, and if you follow their lead during a reading, you'll find that the pieces come together to craft a powerful story throughout their communication to the sitter. When I do have time to ask questions of the spirit, it might be because I'm shifting from one spirit to another during a reading, or perhaps I'm needing a bit more time to understand what's being communicated and I ask a spirit to show me the impression again to make sure what I'm understanding is accurate. This is what I call double-checking my evidence.

While I think it's incredibly helpful to make a list of meaningful evidence that every medium will want to know how to bring through, I also don't allow myself to get too married to any one piece of evidence because I know anything can happen during a reading. Over time, I've found that while it might be sexy to know the year a spirit passed, their name, their exact age, etc., what a sitter really wants is to feel as though they are spending time with their passed loved one. That means that you bring through the essence of their personality and character clearly and accurately. That you understand the relationship between the spirit and the sitter and the dynamics of other relationships that might also be relevant to bring up during the reading. It means that there's a powerful message to be shared that creates an experience for the sitter that is effective in terms of leaving them in a better place than when you found them.

The most joyful way to work as a medium is to enjoy the toolbox that you've got and to continue to work diligently to expand that toolbox so you can be excited when new elements are added. I worked with a student who had a difficult time identifying a spirit's gender and relationship to the sitter but who could always identify a spirit quickly by their cause of passing. She agonized over what she struggled with and took for granted the amazing skill she already had. As we worked together, she secured her ability to identify gender and began to sense the role and relationship of the spirit as well, but her ability to identify the cause of passing remained.

To get you started, or help you continue to expand the pieces of evidence that you bring through, here is a list that helped me consider the most important information to receive about a spirit that also helps to make them identifiable to the sitter. While all of these pieces of evidence are great, I've put an asterisk (*) next to the evidence that I find to be the most powerful during a reading. What makes the starred pieces of evidence more powerful in my mind than those that aren't starred? They more easily lend themselves to identifying the spirit or spirits that you're bringing through with more depth in terms of who they truly were when they were living. For example, knowing their age when they passed may be sexy because it's such a detailed piece of evidence, but it doesn't say as much about them as knowing who is with them on the other side and how much that might mean to the sitter who has survived all of those passed friends and family members who are now together.

Remember that any evidence that gives that depth of identity and makes your sitter feel like they're sitting and having a conversation with their passed loved one will make the reading more powerful. That being said, while I didn't star "hobbies" as one of the most powerful pieces of evidence, for some sitters, it might be! If you were to bring through my mother once she passes and mention our favorite hobby or pastime of boardgames, it would mean *so* very much to me.

As you study these pieces of evidence below, imagine hearing from a passed loved one of yours who you desperately wanted to connect with. What pieces of evidence would be the most meaningful to you?

- Gender*
- Age or age range
- Their role or relationship to the sitter *(side of the family when applicable)*
- Family and friends who are with them on the other side*
- Their death *(details about how they passed like how, where, with whom, and circumstances)*
- Occupation
- Single/Married*
- Family and friends *(specifics about their relationships)*
- Pets*
- Hobbies
- Name
- Where they lived
- Personality/character*
- Foods the liked/disliked
- Buried/cremated
- Interaction with sitter/shared memories*

- Objects/keepsakes
- Birthdays/anniversaries that were/are important to the sitter, spirit, or family members
- Important Events before, during, or after their death*
- Physical description
- The codes or specific conversations/things said/discussed before, during, after death, and prior to reading*
- Message*

A medium brought through a grandfather of mine once during a mediumship course I was taking. This medium was incredible in terms of his accuracy with evidence and the details that he was able to bring through.

Why did I feel so empty when the reading ended then? I realized that most of his evidence was on this list, but very few of the things he shared were starred pieces of evidence. He knew physical descriptions, how many kids there were, what kind of addiction my grandfather suffered from, that he had been divorced once before he married my grandmother, that his marriage to my grandmother was rough and that there was abuse in the family, his occupation, and his age range when he passed.

What he didn't share was a powerful message to me from my grandfather or many details about my grandfather's relationship to my dad and how that had affected me all of my life. In honesty, those were the things I was yearning to hear the most, but they never came. Never forget that sexy detailed pieces of evidence alone do not make a reading. I promise you that your sitter is looking for so much more.

07
Confidence

I can't think of many passions or professions where having confidence *isn't* helpful. We tend to perform best at the things we enjoy, and the things we enjoy tend to be things that we're good at. When you're good at something, you usually have more confidence. It all makes sense, right? When it comes to mediumship, I don't just find confidence to be helpful though, I find it to be a *must*.

One of the largest tasks for any medium is to develop a deep level of trust in both themselves as a conduit and in Spirit. The subtlety of spiritual impressions can lead us to doubt our mediumship. This, in turn, weakens our connection to a spirit during a reading, which can turn spirit communication into a real shit show, and fast. Regular practices that help us to adapt to the challenges of mediumship are so freaking essential I just can't emphasize it enough. As you give more and more readings, I promise you'll have some real doozy experiences. It's unfortunate, but a reality. If you can learn to maintain a high level of confidence regardless of who sits with you or what evidence you're presented with, you'll have a much better time navigating the peaks and valleys of the confidence roller coaster that *all* mediums go through. If any medium tells you they haven't experienced those valleys, I can assure you that they're full of shit.

The question every medium asks when they first begin and even after they've been practicing for a while is: "Am I making this up? Or is this really from a spirit?"

I'll never forget the first time that I ever sat in a development circle. First, I felt like I was a moment away from shitting my pants for the entire ninety minutes of class. Then, as I started sharing "what I was getting"—which felt like the most subtle hints of a bullshit story from my imagination—I remember looking around and thinking, "What the fuck am I doing? Are we all so bored with life and insane that we just like to sit around with each other and make up batshit crazy stories about fake dead people?!"

It takes time and experience to understand how *you* work as a medium. Only after you've spoken with Spirit a number of times, you will become used to the subtleness of impressions and the way you tend to receive information. As you continue your work, you can and will become attuned to the sensation of blending with Spirit. You can and will begin to learn the language of spirit communication if you make continuous effort.

Remember what I shared in chapter five, Becoming a Clear Channel for Spirit, about telling the difference between a thought from your own mind and a thought that is being communicated from a spirit. A thought from a spirit will feel as if it's just dropped into your mind. It won't often be connected to your own personal recent thoughts or experiences because it won't be recognizable as a thought of yours.

You can also use my tools of resonance and dissonance that I shared earlier when you want to feel more confident in the evidence you're receiving. To become more familiar with the feeling of resonance, close your eyes and say something to yourself in your mind that is an absolute truth. For example, I could close my eyes and say, "My name is Mel Pharr" or "I'm married to Rob, and we live in Colorado." These facts are indisputable, and when I say them to myself in my mind, I get that feeling of resonance in my body. Next, say something in your mind that is not true, like, "My name is Barbara Berkshaw" or "I love eating cockroaches, especially when they're still alive and I can feel them wriggling around in my mouth." Hopefully both of those statements gave you a feeling of dissonance, especially the one about cockroaches. Get used to these feelings of resonance and dissonance to help you feel more confident not just in mediumship, but in life when it comes to clearly sensing your own inner knowing. I promise you it'll work wonders for your confidence! Now let's dive into some of the most powerful tools and practices that I use and teach to my students to help them develop the confidence that mediumship requires.

The Power of Intention

I can't overstate just how potent and effective the power of intention is. We live in a vibrating universe where like attracts like. Words and thoughts matter because they set intentions, often without us even realizing it. The way you talk about yourself and your skills as a medium or how you think your next reading is going to go sets you up for success or failure. I get that intending something strongly doesn't always get you the result that you want, but I do know that how we think and what we say directs our actions and our responses. Our actions and responses dictate the kind of experiences we have as we go through this life. One of my favorite quotes of all time is by Wayne Dyer, who said, " If you change the way you look at things, the things you look at change."

What we focus on is what we see more of. Setting an intention is like focusing the lens of your mind. Focus on the things that you'd like to see shift and change with your mediumship practice. Set intentions before you sit with Spirit, practice mediumship, and give readings that focus on what you'd like to accomplish and experience.

I'll share with you a part of my opening prayer that I say before *every* reading. "Spirit, help me to bring through an easily recognizable passed loved one who is a fantastic spirit communicator and easy for me to understand. Help me to bring through a vast body of indisputable evidence so that my sitter *knows* that you are here." I rarely experience readings where my sitter doesn't recognize the spirit that I bring through because this strong and consistent intention that I share before every reading has slowly filled me with confidence in myself and trust in Spirit.

Using the Power of Intention with Confidence Affirmations

Practice using language that sets a powerful intention in terms of growing your confidence. Below I've listed my Mediumship Affirmations for Confidence:

- *I am more able to believe in myself and my mediumistic abilities every day.*
- *Each day, I can say with more confidence that I have mediumistic abilities.*
- *I trust the unfolding of my mediumship journey.*
- *I trust the path of my development as a medium.*
- *I am trusting Spirit more and more each day.*
- *I am allowing myself to be curious and excited about my own unique style of mediumship.*
- *I trust the moments of uncertainty and doubt as powerful teachers along my journey.*
- *I know and intend that out of my doubt and fear of getting it wrong, stronger confidence will be born within me.*
- *I trust that my accuracy as a medium will only grow as I work to develop my craft.*

- *I know that a deeper understanding of the language of spirit is unfolding within me each moment as I move forward on my mediumistic journey.*
- *I feel my awareness expanding each day and each time I channel Spirit.*
- *I am remembering more and more that mediumship is not about focusing on my faults, but about connecting to a powerful, loving energy that heals.*
- *My energy before each reading is becoming more relaxed and more open.*
- *I am peacefully filled with the excitement of Spirit.*
- *As I sit to give a reading, I trust and I know that Spirit always shows up.*
- *I am noticing more and more that as I sit to give a reading, I'm filled with confidence and the knowledge that I will make a positive and healing impact on my sitter.*
- *I feel myself becoming more and more confident in myself as a medium.*
- *I know that I am on this journey for a reason, and I trust that Spirit will help me to develop in a way that allows me to do my best work and be happy.*

To experience these Mediumship Development Confidence Affirmations in a guided video, use this QR code:

Trusting Yourself (and Spirit)

Not all of us think of trust as a skill that builds confidence, and that makes sense. Many people have been in extremely difficult situations that have caused them to lose trust in other people. We often view trust as something that someone else who is in a relationship with us has to earn. While this is true, losing trust in others is often a reflection of trust that has been lost within ourselves. It's just one aspect of trust, but I list it here as a skill because I believe in regard to mediumship, it is. In the practice of mediumship, trust is something that you can practice in a practical way, and as you become precise at recognizing dissonance and resonance within yourself, dissonance and resonance can act as a check and balance system, along with the response of your sitter. In the context of mediumship, practicing trust looks like stating and committing to saying this before you communicate with a spirit: "Whatever I receive, I will trust it's real and coming from Spirit." If you're wrong or your interpretation is off, so be it. You'll discover that soon enough and learn faster along the way. We hinder our learning process when we don't have the trust, courage, and confidence to give to the sitter what we're getting from the spirit because then we never really know how accurate, or not, we were. Below I've shared two exercises that will help you to focus on and strengthen your trust within yourself, and with Spirit.

Exercise #1: Practice Readings that are Audio Only

Many of my readings started out in person. Eventually I shifted the majority of my work online via Zoom. I can see my sitters when I read for them, and I enjoy having that connection. It's important to be able to read well when you're seeing your sitter either in person or on screen because in the long run, you'll be in many situations where this is the case. That said, being able to see your sitter can interfere with your focus on your connection with Spirit if you don't feel that you've built a solid level of trust in yourself and in Spirit. Let's say that the look on your sitter's face is distracting or intimidating while you read. Maybe they are one of those tricky sitters who responds in a confusing way. It's easy during a reading to become derailed due the response or look of your sitter. Practicing giving readings that are audio-only can be a great way to develop your mediumship and keep a strong focus on the connection you have with a spirit. In my mediumship development circles, we practice giving readings in this way regularly so that our focus is almost entirely on our clair senses and our communication with a spirit. Find someone who is willing to sit with you for a practice reading. Make sure that they are clear about the fact that you will not be able to see them, only to hear them, and that they should give a clear "yes," "no," or "maybe" response when you bring through evidence and then ask for validation.

Exercise #2: Practice Readings Where the Sitter Doesn't Respond

Just as practicing a reading with only audio helps you to focus on your connection with the spirit, practicing a reading where the sitter doesn't respond has a similar effect. It adds a little more pressure because you can still see your sitter, but because they aren't responding, there's no reason to divert your focus from your connection. A lot of the practice readings that my students do toward the beginning of a class are readings where the sitter is instructed not to respond. Instead, the sitter will give feedback when the reading is over, and my students are usually pleasantly surprised at their level of accuracy.

How To Prepare for Your Readings

How you approach a reading has great potential to set you up for success. My short and sweet piece of advice is to do for yourself whatever makes you feel confident and comfortable in a very short period of time, a couple of minutes at most. I'm not a fan of needing to follow elongated rituals or detailed to-dos in order to get yourself into the headspace. Why? The more you rely on those types of things, the more you'll *have* to rely on those things to give great readings.

I like to keep things simple. I sit in the power for about five minutes leading up to a reading. You may not be surprised that before I go to sit, I set an intention. It usually sounds something like this: "Spirit, help me to turn any fear and anxiety into confidence and excitement. Help me to focus on the experience of my sitter and give them a reading that is a positive experience and provides them with joy, healing, and peace." I will sometimes add in any intentions I have around the kind of evidence that I'd love Spirit to share with me when I'm working on certain aspects of my mediumship practice. In addition, I am always well hydrated before a reading, and I avoid sugar, dairy, and gluten the day of. That's about it for me. In fact, I like to make sure I'm *not* relying on anything elaborate to get me ready for a reading.

I promise you there will be times where you don't have time to do much preparation because life, and shit, happens. I have grown my confidence by massive amounts realizing that I can read at the drop of a hat, when I have a bad cold, when my stomach hurts, or even *most* of the time I was on Zofran three times a day and still throwing up with morning sickness. I remember giving a reading when the person had yardwork—that included chopping down parts of a tree with a chainsaw—in their backyard or the time I read for a dad whose baby was chewing on the side of his face for about thirty minutes. That's not to say that I don't tell my clients to show up without distractions. I won't read for someone who is multitasking or driving in their car, etc., but when your sitter is present and eager to hear from Spirit, yet things happen outside of their control, you'd be surprised how quickly you can connect.

Preparing for Your Readings Brainstorm

Sit in a quiet and comfortable place where you can take some time to just be. Spending a few minutes meditating may be helpful. Use your laptop or a journal to brainstorm some ideas that come to you about how you can quickly prepare for a reading in a way that makes you feel calm and confident. Once you have an idea of what your preparation looks like, use this before you work mediumistically, and see if you feel that it's setting you up in a powerful way for your readings. You don't have to put a lot of pressure on this process. This is an exploratory process that may change as you progress. It's also an effective way to set yourself up for the best experience before a reading.

How to Handle Hearing "No"

Hearing a "no" when you're just beginning is one of those things that can terrify a new medium right out of their pants. The fear of hearing "no" can be a negatively controlling force over a medium. If there's one thing that's worked really well for me in life, it's to welcome my fears by staring them straight in the face. It's wild how quickly they lose their power when they're pulled out of the shadows and brought into the light. That includes the fear of hearing "no."

The biggest mistake that I see mediums making when they hear "no" is that they *instantly* make the assumption that this response means they are wrong about the evidence they've brought through. Of course, this reaction is rooted in... can you guess? A lack of confidence, one of our most important Cs from the Mediumship Development Framework!

The silver lining is that this tendency to assume we're wrong leads us to ask a better question. What does it *actually* mean when we hear "no" from our sitter? Having a better understanding of the slew of possibilities is so empowering, and it helps us as mediums to shift our focus back where it *should* be, on our communication with the spirit, and on the experience of our sitter.

What are the most common reasons that we hear "no?"

1) Our interpretation of the spiritual impression is off.

Some clairs require more interpretation than others. For example, clairvoyance can require much more interpretation than clairaudience. If you see a picture of a plane, there are a lot of different things this image could stand for. If you hear "dad," that's pretty straightforward.

Because spiritual impressions are one single thought at a time, it's easy for a medium—especially one who is in the beginning stages of development and getting impressions more slowly—to jump to interpretation before receiving the next impression that may bring more clarity or leaning into the impression to see if they sense the meaning that accompanies it. Even for mediums who have been practicing for some time, it's incredibly easy to interpret an impression that is real and legit in an incorrect way, to which the sitter will then say "no."

For example, I remember a reading I gave where the spirit was giving a funny description of themselves as being a muscle man. When I shared this with the sitter, they crinkled their face with confusion and said "no." As I leaned into the impression more, I realized that the spirit had gotten extremely slender before passing, especially in their arms, and was never a muscular person to begin with. They were, however, a jokester with a great sense of humor. They were joking that on the other side, they had muscles. It was a funny way to show they were happy, healed, and at peace. Not only that, but the sitter confirmed that this was the same joke they made when they were still living.

2) The sitter doesn't remember, aka Sitter Amnesia.

If you've given lots of readings, you know that sitters usually listen very intently to what a medium is bringing through. They don't want to miss anything, and every word we say holds great meaning for them. Often, they may be nervous about who might come through or not and what they may or may not say. This, accompanied with their level of focus on what we're saying, doesn't always leave them with the full capacity to remember certain people, events, or details. I've seen it happen a million times, and it's happened to me as a sitter too!

During a reading, I kept getting the name "Jerry" over and over again. The spirit was telling me this was someone that was close to them, and it felt to me as if Jerry had passed. The sitter continued to say "no." The other evidence I'd brought through resonated with the exception of this name. We couldn't figure it out during the reading. My sitter emailed me a week later to let me know that Jerry was a close friend of their father's who had passed away. We finally understood that her father, in spirit, was letting us know that he was reunited with his close friend Jerry.

3) The sitter's mind is focused on a different spirit, person, time, or event.

Before I give a reading, I always educate my sitter briefly about how mediumship works and what they can do during the reading to have the best experience possible. I ask them to do one of the most difficult things as a sitter: to let go of expectations of who might show up and what they might say. This can help them to keep an open mind and not be focused on a particular spirit, person, time, or event. Still, this tight focus of the sitter can happen and sometimes requires more work from the medium so that the sitter can make the connection.

During a class I was teaching, a student's first piece of evidence about a spirit they were bringing through was that this spirit was the sitter's cousin. The sitter confirmed they did have a cousin in spirit. As my student described the personality and character of this cousin, the sitter continued to say "no." She told me she felt stuck, so I linked into the spirit. I could tell she was with a woman who had passed before her time and was recognizable to her sitter, but the spirit didn't feel like a family relation to me. I told her to go back to her sitter and recap the personality and character traits that felt the most significant to her as the medium, asking her sitter if these pieces of evidence could apply to another passed loved one of hers who wasn't her cousin. Sure enough, the nos turned to yeses, and the sitter confirmed that this passed spirit was not her cousin but a close friend of hers. Sometimes a single piece of evidence that isn't quite right can close our sitters mind off to finding the evidence we are bringing through as recognizable.

There was another time in class where a student was bringing through a man who was a close friend of their sitter. The student was sharing that the spirit was seen leaving his house and returning on the same day that he died. The sitter kept saying "no." My student felt stuck, so I jumped in to share that I was understanding that the spirit wasn't talking about himself. He was talking about his awareness of the sitter leaving her house to see him before passing and then returning that evening. The sitter confirmed that this was significant to her and made sense. My student was getting a real and legit impression from the spirit, she was just attributing it to the spirit instead of her sitter.

4) The sitter is unaware of the evidence we are bringing through.

Spirits like to bring new understanding and awareness to their sitter to provide healing and peace, but sometimes the information they bring through to provide this new perspective isn't always information that the sitter is aware of. I gave a reading where the grandparents of my sitter came through. As I described their personality and details about an accident that her living mother had gone through, which her grandparents were referencing, I was hearing "yes." When her grandparents shifted to speaking in detail about her parents' relationship and the effect that this had had on my sitter growing up, I started to hear all nos. I felt confident with what I was getting, but for the remainder of the reading, I didn't get a single "yes" from my sitter. Usually I'll end a reading if for some reason I can't make a connection or bring through evidence that connects after ten or fifteen minutes tops, but because we were further into the reading before the nos began, I went for it and finished the entire reading. I could tell my sitter was emotional and extremely disappointed by the end. I felt horrible. It didn't feel like refunding or rescheduling was the right thing to do, strangely enough, as this is often my response when every once in a while the shit hits the fan. Instead, what I heard from Spirit was to check in with her in forty-eight hours. I said to her, "I understand you're really disappointed, and I'm so sorry. I'm not quite clear what happened during the reading, but do I have permission to check in with you in forty-eight hours, and we'll decide what's best at that point? I have a feeling we need to let this settle in for a bit." She was very upset, but graciously agreed. I was about to reach out to her over email when I noticed a message from her on Instagram that said, "You were right about everything. I just didn't know you were." It turns out that after the reading, she shared what had come through with her parents. They confirmed everything I had said and filled her in on a whole slew of relationship dynamics that she had had no clue about!

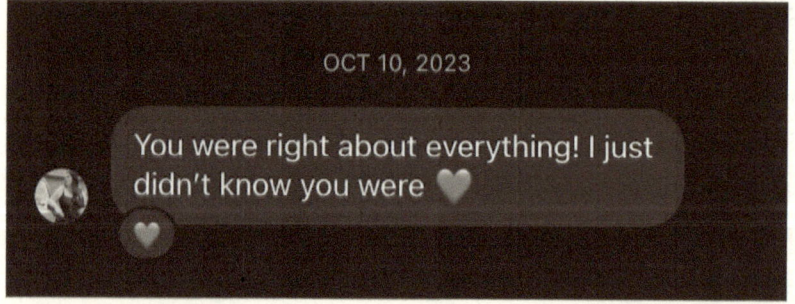

I had another reading that I was hesitant to do because it was for a friend of mine, and I often don't read for friends and family. The circumstances were such that I really felt compelled to give the reading and that it would go well. At one point, the spirit I was bringing through for my friend showed me a gold chunky ring. I told him that it reminded me of a class ring, but it wasn't. He looked confused and said, "I'm not sure. Maybe, but I don't think so." I could see the ring clearly, so I told him to check into it if he could.

He said he would, but he didn't seem convinced. A day later I received this text from him:

The spirit I had brought through for my sitter was a dear friend of his. He had called this passed friend's daughter and asked her if she knew anything about the ring I had mentioned. She burst into tears, telling him that she had found her father's ring among his things three weeks prior and had been wearing the ring every day since. Then she texted him a picture of the ring, which he sent to me. I recognized it instantly.

5) The information we are bringing through is related to something that hasn't taken place yet.

In a mediumistic reading, spirits might communicate about events that have not yet taken place. Sometimes this information is still easily recognizable to a sitter. For example, maybe a spirit references a move that is coming in the future that the sitter knows about or a trip that the sitter is planning to take, or even a book that they've been thinking of writing but haven't written yet. Other times something that is a future reference will not be understood. The same woman who confirmed the personality of her grandparents and the accident her mother had said "no" when I mentioned a brass pin that her grandmother was saying existed. It wasn't for another month, after she had told me I was accurate about many details she hadn't understood about her parents' relationship, that she shared a picture of the pin I had mentioned as well. The message said, "I found it! Now what do I do with it?!"

I told her it was up to her but that Spirit loves to share items or information with us that we discover later as proof of life beyond the death of the physical body. She was thrilled and, I'm sure, held onto the pin as a treasure.

I gave another psychic reading for a client, and although I rarely make predictions, I was getting a strong impression that her eldest daughter would be giving birth to my sitter's first granddaughter in two years time. Fourteen months later, she shared that her daughter was newly pregnant, which lined up quite precisely with the timeline that I had given her.

6) We are bringing through a spirit who isn't recognizable or connected to our sitter or the sitter doesn't know enough about the spirit.

Some of the most frustrating readings can happen when the spirit who pushes through is using your sitter as a messenger to someone living that the sitter has access to, even if your sitter doesn't know a lot about the passed spirit. There are all kinds of situations where a sitter may not have a lot of information about a spirit because they were just an acquaintance, didn't spend much time with them, or passed before the sitter was born or was old enough to recall many details.

I remember giving a reading for a woman whose living brother's living friend's passed mother came through. Yeah, take a second to work that one out. So a woman had a living brother whose friend's mom had passed away. She thought she might know a little about the living friend or her living brother but having any information about her brother's friend's mom was not the case. It was a rough reading, but I was very confident in what I was getting. The most frustrating thing is that she never got back to me about relaying this message, but I share this story anyway because I'm not the first medium who has had this experience.

There was another time that I brought through a great-grandmother during a group reading. As I was describing the great-grandmother, no hands were going up to claim the spirit. I then asked the spirit to give me evidence that would make her recognizable to a sitter. She mentioned a picture that the sitter had, described her long grey hair pulled back into a low bun, and had me make a funny pouting expression. This pouty expression gave the feeling of someone who meant business and was physically and emotionally quite strong and overbearing. Right away, a hand went up. At the end of the reading, the sitter told me that she knew very little about her great-grandmother but that she had that exact picture and had heard stories of her tough, overbearing nature and the fact that she was physically "as strong as an ox!"

What should we do when we hear "no?"

1) Lean into the impression.

Do this by holding it in your mind and allowing it to unfold. What do I mean by this? Remember that spirits send us one thought at a time per spiritual impression. By doing what I call "leaning into the impression," you welcome your other clairs to come in and assist you in your interpretation by working in conjunction with each other. For example, let's say you smell smoke and ask your sitter if they understand their passed loved one to be a smoker. They say "no." You hold that impression in your mind. Clairsentiently you start to get the feeling, and claircognizantly you get the knowing, that they are referencing a fire that happened that caused the death of their loved one. The sitter confirms this.

The other experience that can come from leaning into the spiritual impression and give clarity to you as the medium is that the spirit will send the next spiritual impression that will give more insight into the meaning behind the previous impression. For example, you smell the smoke and get the "no" from your sitter about their passed loved one smoking. As you hold the impression in your mind, you get the image of a house that is burning and realize there was a house fire, which your sitter then confirms. The first impression on its own didn't entirely explain what was being communicated, but as you patiently held it in your mind and waited for the next impression, it came and told more of the story.

2) Ask the spirit one of these two questions, or both.

The first question I ask the spirit when I hear "no" is: "Please give that to me again, if what I'm understanding is what you're trying to communicate." I'm telling the spirit to repeat the impression they sent to double-check my work. I want to make sure it was from the spirit and not something my mind jumped in on. I'll ask the spirit as many as three times to repeat a spiritual impression for me—and not just when I hear a "no." I ask them to repeat impressions when they give me more sensitive information that I want to make sure I get right. For example, I might get my symbol for the spirit taking their own life. I ask for that two to three times so that I'm confident when I bring it through as evidence. There are other times when a spirit will make a reference to infidelity as a way of acknowledging events or apologizing. This is another one that I like to double check. I never immediately make the assumption that I'm wrong when I hear "no," and now you know why. There are numerous reasons we hear "no," and it's our job as mediums to dive deeper into what we're getting instead of moving on quickly and brushing over the evidence. Spirit never wastes a thought. They will communicate evidence in the most efficient way possible.

The second question I'll ask if I'm still unsure of the impression after asking a spirit to repeat it is: "Can you give that to me in a different way?" Maybe the spiritual impression they're giving is more difficult for you to interpret based on your frame of reference. Maybe it leads you to interpret the thought differently than intended or in a way that the sitter can't recognize. Spirit can try giving you the thought in a different way that might make more sense to you.

Let's take the example of when I clairvoyantly saw a beach ball during a reading. I quickly got the sense that this was about a trip to a destination with beaches and sand, but let's say I was confused and I interpreted the beach ball as the spirit liking the beach and got a "no" instead. If I asked the spirit to give me that impression in a different way, perhaps they would show me the image of a plane so that I could understand this was about a trip. Then they could follow it up with the image of an island, and I might be better able to put the pieces together.

3) Cycle through the clairs.

This is one of my favorite mediumship hacks when you feel like you're getting stuck during a reading. Let's say that you're receiving a spiritual impression and it's just not resonating with your sitter. Sometimes this can make us panic or feel pressure and stress. Take a couple of deep breaths, and then start to cycle through the clairs. If the spiritual impression that you were receiving was a clairaudient impression, you could begin by saying, "What do I feel?" See what, if anything, comes through. Then continue on through the rest of the clair senses, "What do I see? What do I taste? What do I smell? What do I know?"

Between each clair, be patient and see what you receive. This is a great way of sensing an additional way, or ways, to interpret what you've been getting. I often do clair-cycling exercises with my students in development circle. I might tell them to bring through the passed loved one of their partner, focusing on *only* three pieces of evidence that they often struggle to get. With each piece of evidence that they are looking to receive accurately, I have them cycle through the clairs to see what clues each different clair might give them. My students are always surprised at just how much more information they receive when they are purposefully opening themselves up to sensing things about that spirit in more ways per piece of evidence. It's all about expanding our spiritual toolbox, and we want to use all of our tools instead of falling into the common trap of bringing through the same old evidence in the same old way.

4) Park the evidence and ask your sitter if they're willing to look into it.

It can happen to *any* medium, no matter how long they've been practicing, that they get stuck on an impression that's coming through, and the impression doesn't seem to resonate with their sitter. I don't let this get to me, especially when the majority of my spiritual impressions are landing and making sense to my sitter. Instead, I just do what we call "parking the evidence." I'll say to my sitter, "I know what I'm understanding is x, y, z, but I get that this doesn't resonate with you, so I'm going to put it to the side for now. We'll see if it comes back or makes sense later in the reading, okay? Would you be willing to make a note of that and look into it with another friend or family member who might recognize what I believe the spirit is trying to say?"

5) Don't let it take you out of the game!

Remember that there are many reasons why you might hear "no" that don't mean that you're not connected to the spirit, not a good medium, not actually receiving a spiritual impression, etc. Don't let a "no" or even *many* nos take you out of the game! The biggest challenge I see most mediums face is *not* that they can't make a strong connection with Spirit, but that they let a lack of confidence take them out of the game before they give themselves a real chance. Nos are inevitable. They are *going* to happen at one point or another, and not just in mediumship, in life! Become unphased by hearing "no," and practice not making it about you.

I had a wonderful client with such potential in my development circle. In a particular class, he struggled to identify a recognizable spirit during a reading exercise and got mostly nos. He wrote me an email after class telling me that he "sucked big time," that "everyone in class brought through spirits" except for him and that he "probably wasn't good enough to be in the class," etc. Then he asked me for advice.

It was clear to me that he had the ability to give powerful readings and to have a strong connection with Spirit. I could tell that he sat in the power often and could feel the blend with Spirit. The common pattern I encountered with him time and time again was that the moment things didn't go perfectly or come easily, he immediately blamed himself, and big time! Not only was he majorly lacking confidence, but the way he talked about himself and his mediumship practice only added insult to injury. I could feel how his energy dropped quickly and significantly at the slightest sign that his sitter didn't understand what he was bringing through, which made it even more difficult to get himself back into the reading.

My promise to my students is that I will always be honest with them, believe in them, and give the kind of support that I believe will help them progress most effectively. I sent a voice memo back to him, saying, "The biggest change you need to make is to your attitude. Spirit is forcing you to change your perspective of yourself and what's possible for you, but until you start thinking about and talking about yourself and your mediumship in terms of what's possible—instead of what you see yourself getting wrong—nothing will change." I give all of my students mediumship affirmations that align with the 5 Cs. I directed him to listen to the Mediumship Development Affirmations for Confidence because sometimes people who have been lacking confidence for a longer period of time need to actually hear different language and wording about how to speak and feel differently. He wrote me back and said, "Wow, I really needed someone to say that to me. I've been listening to the affirmations, and I already sense a change."

To Listen to my Mediumship Development Affirmations for Confidence, use this QR code:

How To Handle Hearing "No" Exercise

I like adding this element to all kinds of practice readings to help my students develop their confidence. Find someone who is willing to sit with you for a practice reading. Explain to them that while they are receiving the reading, no matter whether something resonates with them or not, their only job is to be silent and without facial expression *except* to say "no" when you ask for validation about the evidence you are bringing through. You can do a version where your sitter can validate who the spirit is to them as you begin the reading, but after the link has been anchored, have them be silent except for nos. I will note that this can be difficult for the sitter if the evidence that you bring through is spot on.

The reason this type of exercise can be so effective is that it helps you get used to hearing "no" and, eventually, stop giving the nos so much power. When you know that's what you'll be hearing, you gravitate toward the aspect of the reading that you do have control over, and that is your focus on and connection with Spirit. This is what we always want to focus on during our readings. While it's important to be aware of your sitter and their experience, you're a messenger who can't change the message that a spirit is sending. Give a full reading to your sitter, and at the end, ask them to share feedback with you about what made sense to them about the evidence you brought through and what they didn't understand.

How to Handle a Tricky Sitter

While our priority during a reading is to focus on our connection with Spirit, we do need to be aware of our sitters and their experiences. I am cautious about blaming Spirit or a sitter for the outcomes of my readings. I like to take full responsibility for the quality of my mediumship, and yet, a sitter's energy and response can make reading much more difficult. This is why I find it so important to teach my students how to maintain a high level of confidence no matter who sits with them or what happens during their readings.

There are three main kinds of tricky sitters that I've experienced, although, sadly, this list is not exhaustive. The first is a Chatty Cathy or Chatty Charles. This is the person who loves to talk during the reading. Some of these people just want to be helpful. Some get extremely excited as you start bringing their loved one through and can't help themselves. Other times you may compassionately sense that this person doesn't have many people to speak to, and, as Rob would say, "they have a high word count." Regardless of why they continue to chat during the reading, I do my best to show them lots of patience and compassion. At times I'll let them say a short sentence or two to give them just a little bit of leeway as long as they aren't revealing heaps of evidence that I likely would have brought through.

How to Handle a Chatty Cathy/Charles

A large part of navigating someone chatty comes down to what you say to them *before* the reading begins. You can often tell when you're in this situation before you start. You'll remember that a part of how I prepare my sitters before a reading is to tell them how I work and what they can do to have the best experience. When I get to this part, I emphasize in more detail than usual why it's so important to just sit back and listen, and that when it's time to respond, to please *only* say "yes," "no," or "maybe."

It sounds a bit like this: "To have the best experience possible, it's *so important* that you allow yourself to sit back and just receive what comes through. Your job is just to receive. The *only* time that you'll have to speak at all is when I check in with you about the evidence that's coming through. When I ask if something resonates or makes sense, it's so important that you respond *only* with "yes," "no," or "maybe." The reason this is such a big deal is because you don't want to rob yourself of information that I may potentially bring through. The healing power of mediumship happens when you truly know and understand that your loved one is present and communicating with you because I've shown proof of life by bringing through information that I couldn't have possibly known. In addition, mediums are focusing on their connection to the spirit, so lots of chatting or questions that can potentially jeopardize our focus makes the reading more challenging. We always want you to have the best experience possible. If for any reason you have a difficult time keeping to "yes," "no," or "maybe," I promise I'll help you out and wrangle you!" *(Keep this light and humorous.)* I'll say something like, "Remember, just 'yes,' 'no,' or 'maybe.'"

During the reading, if my sitter talks a lot and starts doing a lot of what we call "feeding the medium," I'll keep my promise by saying, "You're doing great so-and-so, but just a reminder to stick to 'yes,' 'no,' or 'maybe.'" Even if I have to say this two or three times, they usually do quite well after that. When I'm wrangling a Chatty Cathy or Charles, it's about doing everything I can to truly make sure they have a wonderful experience.

I give my sitters about five minutes or so after a reading to speak with me and share about their experience. I always let my sitters know that they'll get this chance to chat *before* I begin the reading. In fact, it's an absolute *must* when you sense that you have a chatterbox on your hands because sometimes they just need to know they'll be able to wag their lips at some point.

How to Handle a Rude Person or an Exceptionally Skeptical Person

It's important to begin by stating that being skeptical does not equal being rude. I myself am pretty skeptical, but I treat all spiritual practitioners with respect. Some extremely skeptical people may come and still give you the feeling that you must prove yourself to them, even if they aren't unkind. Then there are the ones who seem slightly offended by your existence and make comments like, "I've been to several mediums and no one can read me. It's been extremely disappointing."

I group these two together because I handle them the same way. As mediums, most of us can tell when we're in this situation the moment our sitter sits down with us because we can sense their energy. That being said, I don't acknowledge what I sense to be their exceptional skepticism or rude demeanor. I treat them like the nicest person in the world. Unless they use their words to effectively tell me they are in doubt or that I need to prove something to them, I love them up energetically and treat them as innocent until proven otherwise. They have my entire introduction to respond to, to give me a feel for how they might behave during the reading. If I do hear, "If you can't tell me x, y, z, I'll never believe this is true," "I don't really believe in all *this*," the "No one can ever give me good readings" line, etc. I'll respond with, "So-and-so, I just want to stop for a minute and ask you, are you comfortable and wanting to be here and present for this reading?" I give them a chance to respond. If they say something like, "Not really, my girlfriend booked this for me," I tell them, "If you'd like, we can cancel the reading. I'm happy to give you a refund. Mediumship is most effective for someone who is open to the experience."

If they seem like they are at least curious and able to make it through the reading, I'll follow up my first question with, "My job is not to convince or confuse you or make you uncomfortable in any way. I do need to know that you feel prepared and comfortable enough to be open for this reading. If for any reason you're not, there's absolutely no need to stay." I state this with honesty and heartfelt kindness and compassion.

Sitters usually feel pretty nervous before readings about who may or may not show up and what they may or may not say. I do my best to avoid making assumptions about their attitude. Nevertheless, I sweat my titties and pitties off during a reading, not to mention the full-blown swamp twat that occurs due the significant energetic work it takes to give a mind-blowing reading. I'm not available for a sitter to pull the a-hole act on me.

People who hurt often say and do things to hurt others, and so no matter how they behave, my rule is that however I respond to another human has to be in a way that I would be proud of if it were printed on the front page of the largest newspaper in the world. In other words, I take the high road, but I don't go against my boundaries.

How to Handle Someone Who Doesn't Respond or Responds in a Confusing Way

I promise you that at some point you'll experience a sitter who just doesn't respond much or at all. They might just naturally have a deadpan expression or a default resting bitch face. I also include in this category the sitter who responds in a confusing way. It might be that they take quite a while to respond when you present evidence and ask for validation or seem confused about everything you say and even confused about their own response. Then there is the sitter who nods at everything that comes through not because it resonates or they understand, but because they are a natural nodder who is letting you know they are hearing you speak.

Any one of these experiences can make the reading more difficult because the flow of energy can feel like it's starting and stopping. I group these types of sitters together because I handle them similarly.

The bottom line is this: The more confidence you have in your connection with Spirit and the more you move your focus toward the communication you're receiving, the less this will affect you. And yet, when you're checking in with them to make sure that they are understanding what you're bringing through and are having the experience that you intend, you'll need to educate them on how to respond more clearly.

When I'm giving a reading and any one of these above scenarios happens, I'll pause the reading briefly and say something like this: "So-and-so, I'm just gonna pause the reading for a brief moment because I want to make sure what I explained before the reading is clear. Can you please say a nice big 'yes,' 'no,' or 'maybe' in response to the latest evidence I've brought through when I check in with you about whether or not you're understanding it?" Most of the time, people just don't realize that they're not giving you a clear response and then will shift, even if you have to remind them a couple of times.

There may be times when you have to be more specific, for example with the sitter who constantly nods even when they don't understand the evidence. In this case, I will say to the sitter, "I just want to check in quickly because I see you nodding as I speak, but it seems like you might just be nodding to show that you're hearing me, *not* because you're understanding everything that's coming through. Is that correct?" I've gone this route before, and almost every time, the sitter doesn't even realize that they're doing it. I'll kindly tell them, "No worries, but let's shift to a verbal response when I ask for validation, okay? And no need to let me know you're hearing me by nodding your head. Does that make sense?"

With each and every sitter, assume the best and avoid taking anything personally. I don't know ninety-eight percent of the people who sit with me, but I do know that every human has a story. We know so little about another person's experience, and we are quick to make assumptions based on our frame of reference. One of the most soulfully moving lessons that mediumship has given me is the recognition that an aspect of myself can be found in every person I meet. We are not all so different from each other, regardless of the many differences we've trained ourselves to see. Meet people with mercy, compassion, and empathy as best you can, and you'll be pleasantly surprised. No matter how much of a dumpster fire our world can feel in a moment, it remains a profoundly beautiful place in many ways, and it will always benefit from your love and connection.

How to Navigate a Shit Show Reading That Doesn't Work Out

Just as there are multiple reasons that you may hear "no" without it meaning that you aren't a worthy medium, there are multiple reasons the shit might hit the fan. Every once in a while, your reading just doesn't work out.

This doesn't mean you should quit if you feel passionate about doing this work, or that you've lost your ability to communicate with Spirit. Every medium has this experience from time to time, even after they're reached a high level of proficiency and are working professionally. Once again, any medium who tells you this doesn't happen to them is probably full of shit.

I was just beginning my mediumship journey and in the depths of understanding my own mediumship when I experienced my first amazing reading. Shortly after, I experienced my worst reading, which didn't work out. I did a coaching session with my mentor at the time and asked her, "Will I ever have another amazing reading again? What if I'm losing my gift?" She laughed. Clearly she had heard these questions before. She told me the story of going to a renowned place to study mediumship and signing up for a mediumistic reading with a famous medium who was teaching there. This medium had to end the reading ten minutes in because they were unable to make a solid connection and bring through any recognizable evidence about my mentor's passed loved one. "Really?!" I remember being shocked and relieved at the same time.

Another time, I went to a large group reading for a famous medium that I very much respect. This person is incredibly skilled, and every reading I've ever seen online of theirs is very nearly flawless. In the live group reading, I saw them try to make a connection with a sitter's mother and then move on quickly after a minute or two because they couldn't anchor the link and bring through recognizable evidence. This medium is so talented, I figured, they understood that if it wasn't coming in those first couple of minutes as it usually does, then they weren't going to waste time floundering and would serve their audience better by moving on.

When you experience a reading that doesn't work out, do your best not to beat yourself up. It's just not helpful. I promise you that it will only take you out of the game and make your development move slower. Life, and mediumship, gift us unending opportunities to learn. Every experience is rich with potential lessons. Keep in mind as well that mediumship has many unknowns and uncertainties, and sometimes we never really know why things go awry. There are so many reasons that a reading might not work out. Here are just a few of them:

1) The blend with the spirit could be stronger.

Sometimes we just need a stronger connection with the spirit. This can happen if there's anything going on with you as the medium that makes it difficult to raise your vibration. When I had morning sickness so badly that I had to take anti-nausea medication and was still throwing up, it got to the point that I just couldn't read. When I began reading again and wasn't feeling 100%, I promise you I wasn't giving my strongest readings because I couldn't focus as clearly on my connection with the spirits coming through. Another time my connection with a spirit was weak was when I was suffering from crippling anxiety and panic attacks. Negative mind chatter and beliefs can most definitely hinder your connection, as can being sick and not feeling well, feeling fatigued or tired, etc.

2) The intention to connect with a recognizable loved one wasn't set or strongly intended.

Once again, let me stress the importance and power of intention. Spirits are excited to connect with us, and when they see that your "light is on" they *will* come. Your sitter may not know a spirit well, but there may still be a pathway to a loved one of theirs so that a message can be communicated. I strongly recommend making it a habit to set the intention to connect with an easily recognizable passed loved one. Otherwise, the spirit with the greatest need will show up every time, regardless of whether or not they are recognizable to your sitter.

3) You have more than one spirit coming through.

I'll dive into this more in an upcoming section of the book, but it happens often that a medium is getting evidence from two or more spirits and doesn't realize it. A telltale sign of this is when your sitter begins with lots of yeses and then their responses suddenly shift to nos or go back and forth between the two. It's not even that you're not connected or receiving accurate information, instead it's that your sitter is focused on one passed spirit, and suddenly, the evidence isn't matching up with that spirit.

4) Your frame of reference may not match up well with a spirit.

Remember that all spirits work off of our frame of reference. That means they use our knowledge, memories, and experiences to communicate evidence to us. When a spirit wants to get something across that you're unfamiliar with, they'll use what they can to get close, but it doesn't always pan out. A simple example that I can share is when a woman sat with me and a spirit who was a grandmother figure for her came through. This grandmother figure mentioned her deceased lap dog. The spirit was trying to communicate the dog's name to me. She whispered the letter "M" to me and then showed me an image of our local hardware store named Jax. Maybe it should have been obvious to me, but I couldn't figure out what she was saying. At the end of the reading, the sitter told me that her dog's name was Max. Clearly, I didn't put the two together. While Max isn't the most obscure name in the world, it just wasn't in the forefront of my mind and therefore not easily accessible within my frame of reference.

5) All of the same reasons a sitter says 'no' can lead to a reading not working out.

Nuff said.

6) The sitter is difficult to read for, and the medium loses confidence.

We've discussed the main ways that a sitter can be a challenge to read for, but more importantly, it can cause us to lose confidence. What goes hand in hand with losing confidence? A lower vibration. A lower vibration makes it harder to make that solid connection with Spirit.

So what do you do when you've limped your way through a reading and it feels like a gong show? Respond with R&R, baby! That's right, give your sitter two options, a *refund* or the opportunity to *reschedule*. Before I started working professionally, I was extremely nervous to charge money for my readings. I met with a mentor, and I was cringing as I whimpered, "What if it's a shit show? What if the pressure gets to me and then they think I'm a fraud? What if I'm not actually good enough to do this or I'm just making this all up and I'm a nutbar?" I had really needed someone to listen to my worst fears so that I could gain some perspective and have the courage to do what I knew I was ready for.

She did something really helpful. She went along with my worst fears. "Ok, let's say you have a reading that's a disaster. What would you do?"

"Well," I said, "they wouldn't have gotten the service I'd promised, so I'd just give them their money back."

"Great," she smiled. "And you could also offer to reschedule them and give it another shot." I took a moment to let it sink in. Could any single reading really decide my future as a medium? Could any one person, besides me, have that much power over me? Those two thoughts seemed to drop into my mind in a moment, and I believe they were communicated from Spirit, reminding me of the truth. Whether it be mediumship or anything else, no one experience or person could derail me from what I *knew* was my purpose for the foreseeable future unless I let it happen. Life was full of challenges and experiences that didn't go perfectly all the time, I reminded myself.

"What we're doing is taking the pressure off of you by having a backup plan to either reschedule a client or refund them if things don't work out," my teacher said. It didn't make the nerves disappear, but it gave me the strength to move forward.

If the reading feels like it was a shitshow to both me and the client, that's the one that I will refund or offer to reschedule. (Side note that to work professionally, I expect myself and any medium I might hire to have at least a ninety percent success rate with readings and the evidence brought through in a single reading.) If the sitter was pleasant, I will offer them both options. If the sitter was either not pleasant or simply didn't feel like the right fit, I only offer them a refund. When I offer a refund, I additionally add the third R, refer. If they just simply weren't a great fit for me, I'll refer them to a fellow medium I trust. If they were unpleasant, I'll refer them to www.verysoul.com, a site that allows sitters to get free or financially accessible readings.

Seven Ways
To Handle Pressure as a Medium

It's exciting and sometimes frightening to realize that you're receiving signs from and have the ability to communicate with the Spirit World! For those of us who decide to pursue this work and put effort into developing our spirit communication skills, there will quickly come a time when you start to feel the pressure. Mediumship is a huge responsibility. You are giving voice to someone's loved one, and we all want to do our best and get it right! People who come to mediums are often in an emotionally vulnerable state, and some may still be deeply grieving. In the early days of connecting with a spirit for a reading, my heart would nearly pound right out of my chest. It's common for a medium's nervous system to really go to town when we dive into this work. Mediums in general go through a period of time where they are terrified of getting it wrong, and some never learn the tools to handle the pressure and become unphased by hearing "no." If you're passionate about using your skills as a medium, whether professionally or not, you'll most definitely need to master the skill of handling pressure. It can be nerve-racking to give a reading to a partner in a new development circle, to a grieving family, to a single person, or to a group or on a stage! Here are seven different practices that you can start using now to handle the pressure that comes with mediumship:

1) Meditate or sit in the power beforehand.

When my nerves are acting up leading up to readings, I reserve myself ten minutes to sit in the power beforehand. We become accustomed to and comforted by the feeling of sitting with Spirit over time as we practice sitting in the power. This is because we feel confident that we have secured that connection. Try sitting in the power for five to ten minutes, or longer if you need, before a reading.

2) Use the power of intention.

Yes, I'm using the word *intention* again. Before all of my readings, whether I'm feeling nervous or not, I set a clear intention that sounds something like this:

I set the intention that this reading has a powerfully positive and healing effect on my sitter and that it leaves them in a better place than where I found them. I intend to bring through an easily recognizable loved one or loved ones who are fantastic spirit communicators and easy for me to understand. I intend to trust everything that I get from Spirit and to give everything that I get from Spirit. I intend for my confidence to increase as I continue to work with Spirit. I intend to have the tools to remain calm, to gracefully handle whatever comes, and to continue to find joy in this work.

Feel free to borrow any of my words as you set your intention or write down some of your own that make you feel the most calm and confident. Say them to yourself before you meet with your sitter and then release them from your mind.

3) Educate your sitter before the reading.

It is vitally important to educate your sitter before you give a reading, and I can't tell you how many mediums *don't* do this. The first reading I received from a medium went like this: She said hi, told me her name, asked me mine, and started asking me a couple of conversational questions. Those brief questions bled into her giving me lots of psychic advice that I hadn't asked for, but without much context. I had signed up for a mediumistic reading and very much wanted to hear from someone on the other side. She switched to working with Spirit when I asked her to, but then kept going back and forth between working psychically and mediumistically without letting me know when she was doing what. I got something valuable out of the reading, but I wouldn't go back knowing what I know now.

When I educate my sitter, I begin by describing to them how mediumship works. I explain that most mediums work subjectively, meaning that we receive communication from a spirit through thought and that it feels almost identical to paying attention to a daydream. I explain that a spiritual impression is a single thought sent by Spirit via one of the clairs, and I make sure to explain to them that mediums are interpreters and that not all impressions are clear initially in terms of their meaning. I want my sitter to understand that it's easy to misinterpret an impression. I let them know to respond only with "yes," "no," or "maybe" so that they don't "feed the medium" extra information that could potentially rob them of evidence I might have brought through. I also let them know never to feel pressure to say "yes" to anything I bring through and that they can always advocate for themselves by letting me know if something is too traumatic or private to discuss.

There are many misconceptions about mediums. Lots of people think we walk around seeing dead people surrounding a person, and I let them know that this is not the case for most mediums. I share with them that pulling the curtain back on how it all works is something I do so that they feel more empowered and aware of the process. This helps them to feel more comfortable beforehand, and their energy opens up. In turn, it helps me relax, too, because we've established trust as they can feel that I'm genuinely there to help them.

If there is anything I'm particularly nervous about, I *might* transparently share it with the sitter. For example, after being so ill with morning sickness, I went back to giving readings, but I'd taken a bit of time off. I was still taking Zofran to get through my readings and not feeling great, so my confidence was lower than normal, and my nerves were acting up. I added this at the end of my educational explanation: "I'm going to share some private information with you that I'd like you to know. I'm fifteen weeks pregnant, and I've been very ill. I share this because previously I was unable to read due to being so sick. I wouldn't have shown up for today's reading if I didn't think I could provide you with the service that I promised. That being said, I just want to make you aware of my situation; so if for some reason I can't connect well, know that I'll reschedule you as soon as possible so that you get what you've been promised."

Many times I don't mention disclaimers that have to do with my nerves because I don't find it particularly professional. It certainly wouldn't make me feel confident if I were the sitter, and it's not something that I want to hear. In general, buck up and keep it to yourself so the sitter can have the experience they deserve. But, if you're going through something that, if named, might relieve a massive amount of pressure, think about how to word it professionally so that your sitter doesn't lose confidence in you, but understands the season you're going through. Write out what you might say to educate your sitter before a reading. Think about what you feel is most important for them to know so that they have a good experience and so that the reading is easier for you as well.

4) Create a calming physical cue.

This is a powerful practice that I use during my readings when I start to feel pressure or my confidence feels shaky. I'm sure if you haven't yet, you will have a moment where an impression comes that doesn't feel clear and you start to feel a little agitated or panicky. This is a sign that your nervous system is acting up and that it may be helpful to have a physical cue that you can use to calm it back down. My therapist told me once that taking three slow, deep breaths can act as a reset for the nervous system. While I don't stop during a reading to take three deep breaths very often, here are some of the physical cues I do use that help me a lot. My favorite cue is placing my right hand over my left and pausing to take one slow, deep breath. There's always time for that, and for me, it definitely provides a moment to ground myself. I will also just focus on taking deep breaths as I'm waiting for impressions. It doesn't look to my sitter like I'm pausing the reading to take slow deep breaths, but I'm doing it as I patiently wait for the next impression that might clear things up. Another physical cue that works well for me is to physically lean back in my chair and put a hand on my heart. This helps to ground me and get me out of any energy that feels panicky or desperate. You can try any of the cues that I've shared, or you can come up with your own. Remember that different things work for different people, so don't become frustrated if what I do doesn't work for you. You can always sit with Spirit for a few moments and ask what physical cue might bring you peace and confidence during a moment of nerves.

5) Ask the angels, your guides, or your passed loved ones for help.

This is something simple that you can do before or even during a reading. Maybe you feel like you have a strong connection with angels, your spirit guides, or your passed loved ones and you ask them to support you with your intention to remain calm and confident while you work. I include an ask to all three of these groups during the spiritual prayer that I say before I begin my readings. It sounds like this: "I'm calling on the angels, my spirit guides, and my passed loved ones to be with us during this reading. Please bring us lots of energy that we can use to have a positive, healing, and powerful experience today." If I say the prayer out loud, or even if I don't—based on my sitter's preference—I also include their spirit guides and their passed loved ones. In a moment of uncertainty, when I feel my confidence wane during a reading, I rely mostly on physical calming cues. If I were to call upon these groups during a reading, I'd simply take a deep breath and within my mind I would ask for their support to guide me and give me clarity, calm, and confidence. Is this something you might try? If so, write down a sentence or two to call upon other spiritual entities who might assist you with your mediumship.

6) Don't let yourself be rushed.

It's easy to feel like you have to be quick when you read. Maybe you've watched other mediums who read more quickly or in a flow state. Take the pressure off, and remind yourself that there's no need to rush. While long periods of silence are not preferable, if you need the time, let your sitter know beforehand that there may be longer periods of silence while you confirm what you're receiving before presenting it to them. I remind myself that it's my job as the medium to not allow myself to be rushed. If I get a little confused or frustrated during a reading, I slow down and take a deep breath or give myself the time to use a calming physical cue. Take the time that you need when you're too unsure to do the work a medium must do. That means leaning into impressions and letting them unfold so that you can communicate more accurately. It takes courage and confidence. As you get to know the language of Spirit better and better, it will become easier to read with more efficiency. Keep in mind as well that sitters can only process so much information, so slowing down for some of us who read quickly is important as well. As a sitter, hearing from your passed loved ones is a lot to take in!

7) Are you energetically receiving or reaching?

You want to be able to become aware of yourself energetically while working with Spirit in terms of whether or not you are in a receptive state. I teach my students that we want to be in a *receiving* state while reading and avoid what I call a *reaching* state. The receiving state happens when we are calm and collected with a clear mind. It feels as though you are even energetically leaning back a bit. Sometimes I do lean back physically in my chair when I read to remind myself that Spirit is sending impressions to me and that I'm simply receiving them. I imagine them floating straight into my mind without effort on my part. This is because one of the hardest parts about being a medium is just getting yourself out of the way. You're simply a messenger. The reaching state is exactly what it sounds like; it's when you're energetically reaching or feeling a grasping energy between impressions or even as you interpret them. It's an energy that feels desperate to sense the next impression and hear "yes" quickly. Mediumship becomes more and more elusive the harder we try.

Think about how easily spiritual impressions came to you when you were first coming into your gifts and how spontaneous they felt. Spirit will often try to communicate with us in our most relaxed state, like while we're taking a shower, falling asleep, or waking up.

This idea of being in a receptive energy works well for many people, and whether you are more Spirit-lead when you read or whether you interview Spirit doesn't matter. It's a passive thing to be a clear channel and give a mediumistic reading.

08
Community

Developing your mediumship can be quite the lonely road at times. While some of us are lucky enough to have family and friends who are open and supportive, others are entirely alone on their journey. They may even feel that pursuing their spiritual gifts could threaten some of their most important relationships.

While mediumship is much more accepted today than it was in the past, there are still many people who believe that speaking to Spirit is an evil act or threatens their own belief systems. Even if you do have family and friends who are accepting and supportive, it can feel isolating if you don't have someone to talk to about your work who gets it.

Having a community can also be an incredible aspect of helping you develop your craft. In classes of mine, my students constantly share stories, wanting to know if anyone else has had similar experiences. I can see how comforted they are to know that they aren't alone. Other times I see students feeling massively liberated to know that every medium works differently. This gives them the freedom and joy to explore their own natural path of development and to let go of comparison or trying to work like someone else. Another major advantage of developing with friends and a community is having plenty of people to practice with in a safe and encouraging environment. While not everyone develops community and mediumship friendships in the same way, here are the most powerful ways that I've found to surround myself with support that has catapulted my mediumship to the next level:

Make Friends with Other Mediums

I went through the initial part of my mediumship journey without a medium friend. Luckily, I had plenty of friends who were spiritually open and excited about my new endeavors. My husband and parents were incredibly supportive as well. Still, there were many moments where I felt alone and isolated. As wonderful as these people were, they didn't really understand what it was like to *be* a medium. What I really yearned for was someone to talk to who was having similar experiences or who at least knew what I was talking about and didn't think of mediumship as a wild and strange thing.

Thank Spirit that I went to study at Arthur Findlay College shortly after I became aware of my mediumistic abilities. My first week at Arthur Findlay College was one of the best weeks of my life, and the friends I met there are incredible people who I still talk to on a regular basis. One of them in particular is a friend who I text with every single week. I can't tell you how many times we've discussed our unfolding abilities, our wins, and our shitshow readings that happen every now and again. We've cheered each other on countless times, encouraged each other when we're down, and simply enjoyed feeling like normal people together because we can talk about our work without feeling like we're censoring ourselves or having to explain. We've also practiced mediumship exercises together, referred clients, and introduced each other to more medium friends.

To me and to so many of my students, these friendships are priceless. While we definitely feel the loneliness of isolation, we don't always notice just how powerful this kind of support is while we have it. Your friend might be the reason you have the confidence to give a great next reading when the one before was an absolute struggle. If you're like some of the students I've spoken to who have had a rough experience with a tricky sitter that makes them feel like giving up their work as a medium, you might be the friend who helps them find a perspective that keeps them in the game. My mediumship bestie found us the best mediumship class I'd ever taken, and we flew to the event and spent the week learning together. It became one more week of doing what I love that I'll never forget.

Making Medium Friends Exercise: Part I

Our thoughts are powerful things that I truly believe help us to create our own future. When I'm looking to create anything in my life, I always work to get clarity about what it might look like. For me, finding powerful friendships is no exception. Make a list of the qualities you're looking for in your medium bestie and what you'd love to get out of the relationship. Here's a quick example below:

Quality	What I'm Looking For in a Friendship
Kindness	Someone with a high level of skill in mediumship
Honesty, transparency, integrity	Someone who is committed to advancing their skills
Generosity of spirit	Someone who inspires me by their skill and integrity
Humor	Someone to practice mediumship exercises with
A good listener	Someone who has a growth mindset and loves classes
Available time-wise & emotionally	Someone who can travel to meet me at events
Passionate	Someone I could partner with onstage in group readings
Driven & confident	Someone who is thinking about or writing a book

Try making your own list of qualities that are important to you and what you're really looking to get out of an awesome friendship with another medium or mediums!

Making Medium Friends Exercise: Part II

Now that you've got clarity about what you're looking for, it's time to put yourself in different environments that make it more likely you'll meet people who might become great friends over time. The list below is not exhaustive. There are many places you could go to find mediumship friends and other fellow spiritual practitioners. Take some time to do research in your area about a couple of the places listed below and plan over the next month or ninety days to experience these environments and see how it goes!

- Mediumship conferences or events
- Mediumship classes online
- Spiritual meetups (try meetup.com in your area)
- Spiritualist churches
- Meditation circles
- Women's circles
- Men's circles
- Spiritual retreats
- Start your own mediumship community

Get Guidance from a Great Teacher

Having a mentor or teacher to guide you along the way can be a powerful aspect of your mediumship unfoldment and your spiritual community. I've never had a teacher that I agree with on every single aspect of mediumship. Sometimes when we're looking for a mentor, we think that we have to be in lockstep with them about just about everything. I've found that it's more important to have them share my values and my vision. Diversity in our thinking is something that often helps me stretch myself in new ways as long as those other two things are in place.

Let's talk first about the many potential advantages of having a great mentor. A great mentor should be able to sense and read into many things about your work as a spiritual practitioner to help give you valuable clarity. They should be able to sense when you are blending with Spirit so that they can validate for you any tell signs and let you know when you are actually connected to Spirit. They should also be able to read accurately into *how* you work. This might look like being able to validate or clarify which clairs are most dominant for you, special or unique opportunities they see for you as a spiritual practitioner, and any challenges they may foresee as well. They should be able to read you psychically to see exciting aspects of your potential mediumship style and identity and behaviors or triggers that might hold you back.

A great mentor will often be able to help you sort out what might have happened when a reading didn't work out well even if they weren't present for the reading. They can also help to normalize the mediumship cycles that we all go through and give perspective. I didn't realize that our mediumship moves in cycles when I was first developing, so when I felt like my practice took a step backward before it jumped forward again, I was a bit anxious, and my mentor helped me to relax.

With a mentor, you get to spend time speaking to someone you trust who has gone before you and likely has some awesome hacks that will help you move further and faster. There is much to be discovered simply from experience, but putting the pieces together from our experiences usually takes a lot longer than having someone who is more advanced give us some clues that are not always so obvious to us. Great mentors are always people who can be a sounding board along your journey and who you can share ideas and experiences with as well.

The question is: How do you find a mentor that you resonate with, trust, and who has all of these skills? You have to know what to look for and where to look. Below I've shared what I look for in a mentor and how I've found my favorite ones.

What to Look For in a Great Teacher

1) Someone who you respect as a medium

I don't know about you, but the people I want to learn from are people who already have the skills that I'm passionate about developing. That means that I make sure I've seen them work and that I value and respect their skills. While there's nothing wrong with learning from someone who is just a couple of steps ahead of you, I like to learn from someone significantly advanced because I feel their depth of knowledge has a greater impact on my ability to grow further and faster.

2) Someone who gets rave reviews via referral or your own research

One of my favorite and most impactful mentors was someone I found in a Google search. I looked at her website and saw that she had vast experience, was featured in the media, and had absolutely rave reviews. I was able to follow her on Instagram, and I enjoyed her personality. When I signed up for her development circle, she blew my mind. I had massive respect for her and found that she was excellent at her craft. In addition, she was one of the most effective and fun teachers that I'd ever had. The other way that I found great mentors was by looking up mediums who had taught, or were currently teaching, at some of the most reputable places to study mediumship, like the *Journey Within Spiritualist Church*, the *Arthur Findlay College*, or the *College of Psychic Studies*. The quality of teaching has always been great. I am not a religious person, however, so learning in a spiritualist setting has not been quite as much of a match for who I am as a person, and I've found that there is sometimes a formal style that doesn't feel like me. All to say that quality of teaching is one thing, and then finding the teacher who is the right fit based on who you are is also important.

3) Someone who clearly understands the mechanics of mediumship and who gives insight and exercises that help you to advance your craft

You'll have all kinds of experiences when you're speaking with Spirit. I've worked with teachers who didn't really know what to make of a challenging reading I tell them about, but I've had a good handful who instantly recognized what had happened and were able to provide insight as well as techniques to maneuver the situation should it happen again. For example, my best mentors knew how to recognize and handle situations like identifying when there are multiple spirits present, what to do when the evidence you bring is only recognizable for a living person, how to understand whether evidence is symbolic or literal, how to link in with the same spirit that a student is bringing through if you're at the point in your development to teach, etc.

4) Someone who believes that the practice of mediumship can be playful, joyful, and involve humor

I absolutely believe that mediumship is a sacred practice in that it deserves reverence and respect. I also believe that one of the best ways to elicit the great healing power of mediumship is to allow the playful, joyful, and humorous aspects of Spirit to shine through in our work. A spirit may even come to you because a strong aspect of your frame of reference matches up with the joy and humor that they'd like to communicate through you to their loved one. It's easy when we're talking about death to get pretty solemn and grave. Of course there are moments that might match up with those ways, but Spirit usually asks us to celebrate their life, remember meaningful moments, and keep living to our fullest despite the fact that our loved ones have passed on. To me, spiritual work is play and one of the most joyful experiences of my life. I believe that the vibration of joy and humor is what allows me to so easily be deeply connected to Spirit.

5) Someone who believes in you and gives you ample room to develop in your own unique way

Coming into your gifts can be a vulnerable time. If you're speaking to Spirit for the first time, you probably don't know exactly what to expect. Your mind might certainly feel blown. The world starts to look like a more magical place than you've previously believed it to be. This is the high that comes with the discovery of mediumistic skills and one of the many draws that can make you feel like you want to speak to Spirit constantly. You'll also be hungry for answers and desperate to speak with other people who may have those answers or at least be able to speak the same language as you in terms of their experience. It's a time when just about anything and everything can feel like a sign. If you reach out for advice or mentorship, it's easy to take it to heart instead of with a grain of salt. In the early stages, whatever you're told may have a profound impact on your path of development. The challenge is that I've never spoken to any two mediums who share all of the same belief systems about how mediumship works or how it *should* be practiced and developed. That means that during a time when you are deeply searching and questioning, you mustn't forget to know yourself and what's best for you. I haven't found it's important to agree on everything with anybody, even a mentor. Above all, I feel it's a must that your teacher or mentor displays great belief in you and allows you the space to develop in your own unique way. I've spoken with mediums whose first teachers were so rigid about how they were meant to develop or read that their skills seemed to entirely shut down and their passion for this work nearly left them. Mediums who have this experience generally tend to have a lot of unlearning to do, which can feel tedious and like an uphill battle. A teacher who is confident and genuinely invested in helping you won't be threatened by your gift in any way or put off by how your mediumship is pulling you in different directions or developing naturally and uniquely. Instead, they will share your excitement and offer advice to help you that you can take or leave.

6) Don't ever let anyone tell you what's not possible for you with your spiritual gifts or any other aspect of your life, for that matter.

It's as simple as that. What's the point of having someone tell you what they think you're incapable of? The most remarkable happenings are often spontaneous and unexpected. The most miraculous discoveries usually aren't predictable. Consider just how many unknowns there are when it comes to mediumship. Who is to say what is or isn't possible? If you have a deep passion for this work and you feel that pull within you, I say go for it. My journey so far has only shown me that those who are drawn to this work are drawn for a reason. Trust it. With mediumship, you truly have nothing to lose, as I see it, but there is *so* much to gain.

Just as you made a list of qualities for a friend you're looking for, here's an opportunity to make a list of qualities and what to look for in a mentor. You can draw from what I've shared above about the best qualities to look for in a great mentor.

Join a Development Circle

If you're never heard of a development circle before, have no fear. It's what it sounds like, a group of people who work to develop spiritually. There are many kinds of development circles. Circles may focus on psychic development, mental mediumship, trance mediumship, or physical mediumship. There are also circles that focus on connecting with spirit guides, angels, or other cosmic beings. What they all have in common is that they bring people together on a regular basis to focus on their development. There are open groups, meaning that anyone can join when they want, so you're likely to have different people that you're working with each week. There are also closed groups where everyone who shows up (usually every week) are members of the same group.

My Mediumship Development Circles are closed groups, and they focus on helping people develop mental mediumship as evidential mediums. You bet that when I was first developing my skills, I joined my first mediumship development group ASAP. That first development circle I joined was an open group. It was powerful because it served one of the very important purposes that circles do: to be a playground for practicing giving readings on a regular basis in a supportive and low pressure environment. It was so exciting to start sharing what I thought I was just making up and having someone raise their hand to say, "Yes, that's for me, and yes, what you're saying is accurate."

Development circles are, in my mind, a *must* for mediums who really want to take their skills to the next level and be able to provide an incredible experience of healing and connection for the people who sit with them. Having a place to read consistently every single week is one of the top practices that has helped me quickly and vastly improve my mediumship. You are able to make mistakes, get better at hearing "no," see others read, and observe how different every person is as a medium. These experiences are invaluable.

How to Find a Good Mediumship Development Circle

Know your purpose for joining a circle and what you'd like to get out of it. Surprise, surprise! I made a list of what I was looking to get out of a mediumship development circle, and I'm sharing it with you here to give you some ideas.

My purpose for joining a Development Circle:

- To develop a deep and powerful connection to Spirit to help me live a happier and more rich life
- To learn to quiet my mind
- To learn the language of Spirit
- To understand the difference between my thoughts and spiritual impressions
- To find like-minded people who understand and support me
- To feel confident in my psychic abilities
- To feel confident in my mediumship and confident calling myself a medium
- To gain a command of my craft so that I can become a professional evidential medium and do incredible healing work with others
- My overarching purpose that I believe I'm here for is to help bridge the division in our country and in our world.

I suggest making a list of your own so that you feel clear about what you're looking for and what kind of development circle is best for you. Don't forget to think about the culture of the group as well and what qualities are important to you in terms of the community. Here are the things that are most important for me when it comes to finding a great development circle:

1) The development circle community should be a harmonious environment with a positive group culture.

Spirit works best in a relaxed and caring environment. It's no surprise, right? Being stressed and uptight never leads to your best work as a medium. There has to be trust between you and yourself, you and Spirit, and you and the people who surround you for things to flow in an ultimate way. This means that in a circle, you feel welcome, safe, and supported. It's also important to feel comfortable enough to stretch yourself outside of your comfort zone. I constantly remind my students to take risks and to be bold in a circle. It's a much better place to make mistakes because the stakes aren't as high—not to mention that you learn better and faster when you go for it. Another important part of a harmonious environment means feeling genuinely believed in and encouraged. That means that other mediums and the teacher *want* you to succeed and do your best work! Take into consideration the culture of the group as well. What is the feel that you get from the group, and does it match up for you? As I've found my own style as a medium, I've realized that the culture of some development groups is too formal for me. I don't like feeling like my practice of mediumship is a religious endeavor or that I must take on a formal demeanor that just isn't me. I swear sometimes while I work if that's what's being communicated from the spirit or to bring a bit of humor to lighten a heavy situation when appropriate. In other ways that I believe are ethical, I don't filter my message to make people—the sitter or audience—more comfortable if a strong truth needs to be told that will bring profound healing.

2) Solid teaching and structure

I've been teaching in one capacity or another since 2007, and I've found that for people to learn anything well and progress as efficiently as possible, having a certain amount of structure, or a framework, is a game changer! This framework, aka the foundation and mapped out system from which a teacher teaches, must allow for two things. First, the freedom for someone to truly discover their own unique style and identity within their craft. And second, for the student to have an effective roadmap that provides them with a system for how to go about their development. A structure or framework is also, unfortunately, the thing that I often see being left out in the spiritual development world. It is paramount though, especially due to the exploratory and intangible nature of spiritual work and the spiritual industry. I've already introduced you to my Mediumship Development Framework, and this book is taking you through it via the 5 Cs of mediumship: Becoming A Clear Channel, Communication and the Clairs, Community, Confidence, and Command of Craft.

In addition to a framework or structure, you also want someone leading your development circle who is adept at teaching. Just because a medium is good at their craft doesn't guarantee that they'll be a great teacher and a good fit for you. It's important that they can explain things in a way that's easy for you to understand and that they have the mentorship qualities that we've discussed.

3) Good leadership

A good leader is someone who you respect. It's good if you've seen their work and feel they have great skill and that they excel at their craft. They should also have the knowledge to answer your questions or say with confidence when they don't know. A good leader is someone without an ego. This means they consider themselves a lifelong learner and a developing medium and that they practice mediumship as a healing service that isn't first and foremost about them.

A great leader is someone who creates a positive learning environment. This looks like creating clear expectations for everyone in the group. They are someone who is kind. They help you to build your confidence and to stretch outside of your comfort zone. They give you constructive feedback in a way that can be received. It's important that I find someone who is also grounded, and not fear-based or airy fairy. I like my leadership to have two feet on the ground and to realize that we came to this material, physical world to be humans as well as spiritual practitioners.

4) Commitment

A development circle that will give you the most bang for its buck— if your purpose is to advance your mediumship—is most definitely a group that is full of people who are highly committed to their spiritual development. This brings up the two different kinds of groups, open and closed. Remember that with open groups, new people can filter in each week and that with a closed group, the same group meets each week. No way is right or wrong. It depends once again upon your purpose for joining and what you'd like to get out of the experience. I've experienced and enjoyed both types of groups.

I've found that I prefer a closed group. I feel that in a closed group, the people seem to have a higher level of commitment to their spiritual development. I also feel that when you're with the same people, trust builds faster and stronger.

5) Ideal logistics

If you're really looking to excel at your craft, then joining a circle that meets weekly—and most do—is important. There's nothing like knowing that you have a place to read consistently each and every week. For me, the ideal circle is 90 minutes to two hours and has at least eight people, with 16–18 max. Consider whether the group meets in person or virtually. I love a group that meets virtually, whether I'm attending or teaching. The convenience is huge at this stage in my life as a parent with a full schedule. You may find that some of these things are more or less important to you, but regardless of where the group meets, this timing and group size seem ideal for myself and my students in terms of creating the best environment for learning.

Connect with Your Spirit Guides

I can't tell you just how much excitement there is around the topic of spirit guides. Certainly, using "spirit guide" in my key words has done a lot of good on my YouTube channel because it is one of the most searched spiritual phrases. What better time to talk about spirit guides than in the section about community? After all, your guides are an important part of your support as you journey through this life.

What is a spirit guide?

From what I've studied and found through communicating with Spirit, I've come to believe that spirit guides are a real thing, even if we as humans have created an interpretation around whatever these spiritual entities actually turn out to be on the other side. As I understand it, a spirit guide is a spiritual being or entity that offers a human being support, guidance, and protection with the purpose of helping them fulfill their intentions for soul evolution in a particular earth journey.

Does everyone have them?

I do believe that all living human beings have spirit guides.

How many spirit guides do we have?

In my communication with Spirit, I've come to understand that we have a core group of guides who work together to be our main support. I often hear that this core group consists of anywhere between four to nine spirit guides, but that our overall number of spirit guides throughout our earth life is about sixty. It's been very interesting that every time I give a spiritual assessment, I hear this number when I begin connecting with a client's spirit team.

Are there different kinds of spirit guides?

I do believe that different guides seem to specialize in different aspects of support for us. Some mediums go as far as to say that each of us has certain specific kinds of spirit guides. For example, some mediums will say we all have a gatekeeper spirit guide whose main role is to protect our energy and only let certain spirits make contact with us. I can't say that I definitively disagree with this idea, but I haven't had that communicated to me from Spirit, so it's not an interpretation that I feel strongly inclined to believe in. Some mediums will share experiences of having spirit guides help them to facilitate mediumistic readings by "helping a passed loved one to communicate" or "going to find a passed loved one and bring them forward" during a reading. I have heard this quite often but have never experienced it myself. When I want to communicate with a spirit, I just do it, and directly.

I am commonly asked if passed loved ones act as spirit guides. I don't know the answer to this, but I lean toward no. In my communication with a client's spirit guides, I have never recognized family members or friends as guides. I have also read books from many other experienced mediums claiming that spirit guides are spiritual beings who no longer walk the earth. Could this be true, and a reason that passed loved ones aren't often guides? Maybe that's a part of the explanation for why I have never recognized spirit guides as family members or friends. Ultimately, I don't feel that assigning spirit guides into certain categories makes much difference to me, so I don't spend a lot of time thinking about it.

Do we need to know who our spirit guides are?

No, you don't need to know who your guides are. I have never found that having knowledge of your spirit guides makes you more or less effective as a medium, or necessarily more or less effective as a human being. I have found that many spiritual practitioners and mediums put an immense amount of pressure on themselves in terms of knowing who their guides are and how they function. Others don't even notice that they are desperate for answers about their life and will sometimes become obsessed with connecting to their guides for these answers. However, I feel that all spiritual entities that guide us do just that. They *guide* us in the direction of soul evolution, but they leave the decisions and the learning of the lessons up to us. We have free will, and we come into this world with no memory of the past because we are meant to approach our earth journeys with the mind of a beginner. Why? This is what gives us the greatest potential for soul evolution. Spirit and our spirit guides want us to be present in this life and to live fully. That's what we're here for. If we spend our entire lives trying to desperately pry answers out of others, our guides included, I'd bet on them saying something like this when we get to the other side: "Well, you spent all your time with your head in the clouds talking to us, so you're definitely going back. You only crossed about ten percent of the shit you were supposed to do off the list!"

In my experience, your guides will make you aware of them when necessary. Please, take the pressure off *needing* to know who they are and how they help if it isn't coming easily. Alternatively, go to a medium who specializes in communication with spirit guides and let them give you insight.

My personal experience with my spirit guides came when I had absolutely no expectations about what might happen as I began the practice of sitting in the power. I wasn't sitting to meet my guides. I was sitting with the intention of further developing my mediumship skills.

I became aware of four main guides that I felt were close supports for me. One of my most impactful encounters with a spirit guide was when I felt I was being taken through emotional memories of breakups and relationship conflicts throughout my life. I could hear him saying that he had been there with me each and every time, comforting me. I recognized that this spirit guide, whose name I heard as John, was an emotional support spirit guide, and I felt deeply comforted. I also found it incredibly validating when, during a spiritual assessment from a mentor who I deeply trust, she also identified four spirit guides as my core team. Many of the details that I've interpreted were the same as hers. These experiences with my guides happened within the first six months of my development. It was as if they felt it would be helpful for me to have this awareness. Since then, I haven't had additional information come through about them, and I haven't gone looking for it. I have a deep knowing that if and when there's a time that I need to become more aware and knowledgeable of them, I will.

How do you connect with your spirit guides?

The first thing I'll reiterate is to go into these experiences with no expectations and without putting pressure on yourself. This is the time when mediumship and spiritual awareness flows best. I'm sharing three of my favorite ways to connect with my guides below. Be patient with them and with yourself. Trust that your relationship with and your awareness of your guides is as it should be.

1) Follow a guided meditation or sit in the power.

Without expectation or pressure, set the intention to connect with your spirit guide or guides. You can follow a guided meditation to connect with your guides or a guided sitting-in-the-power meditation to connect with your guides. You can also meditate or sit in the power on your own and simply set the intention beforehand that you will be able to connect to your spirit guides in some way. When I became aware of my guides, it wasn't through guided meditation. It was just sitting without expectation and all of a sudden having thoughts and images and new awareness come into my mind. If you do want to feel like you have some kind of structure to follow, you can easily search online for a meeting-your-spirit-guides sort of meditation or sitting in the power experience.

Use the QR code below to listen to my guided sitting in the power meditation, "Sitting in the Power to Connect with Your Spirit Guides," to help you connect with your spirit guides.

You can also visit this video, "*4 Ways To Connect With Your Spirit Guides*," using the QR code below:

2) Automatic writing

Automatic writing is a great way to get in touch not just with your spirit guides but also with your higher self, source, the universe, God, or whatever you want to call the all-one spiritual energy that we are connected to. You can use a notebook to write by hand or a computer. I like using my laptop because it's easier for me to keep up with what comes to mind when typing than when writing by hand. As you sit down to write, set an intention for yourself about who you'd like to connect with. If it helps to ask a broad or more general question, you can do that as well. Maybe it sounds like this: "I'm setting the intention to connect with my spirit guides" or "I'm strongly intending to connect with my guides and my question is, 'What do I need to know today?'"

Keeping it simple is a good way to go. It can be helpful to sit in meditation for three to five minutes before you begin writing if your mind wanders or you feel like it's too active. Once you're ready to begin, start writing by hand or typing without allowing your mind to become active. Just do your best. See what comes to you by letting your hands move, and don't analyze it. A good way to know that you are connected to Spirit is by using words that you don't know the definition of, but once you look them up afterwards, they make sense and are in proper context. You may also feel like the voice of the writing doesn't sound like you or shares wisdom that you weren't aware of before.

You can additionally write in more of a question-and-answer format. You might start with a question of your own, like, "Spirit Guides, are you there?" and then go into the same type of automatic writing in order to get an answer back. No one way is better than the other; it's just about what works for you. Try not to be discouraged if you feel like this is a challenging task. It is one that gets easier over time, and it may require more time quieting your mind before you begin.

3) Ask your guides for a sign.

If you're wanting to experience confirmation that you have spirit guides of your own, you can always ask them for a sign. Chances are they've been sending you signs all your life, but if you're not looking for signs, they can be easy to miss. I find that it's incredibly powerful to ask for something specific from them. Remember how I shared with you that at the beginning of my mediumship journey, I ended up sharing with my friend a message that had come through from her deceased father? When I left her house that day, I was feeling emotional and hoping that I'd done right by her and the Spirit World—if they even existed, which is what I was thinking at that point. I got in my car after putting my daughter in her car seat and sat in the driver's seat with my hands gripping the steering wheel. "Okay spirit guides, if this is all real, if this isn't a load of absolute bullshit, and if I'm not going fucking insane, I need you to tell me. I need you to make it obvious! I need to know that that was the right thing to do, so you've got to give me some kind of sign." Instantly after making my declaration I heard the word "hippo" in my mind.

"Seriously?" I grouchily said out loud, "That is the stupidest idea I've ever heard of. Where the fuck am I going to see a hippo?"

My daughter was cooing in the back seat. I could see her watching me in her little mirror. Maybe she was wondering if mama was going off the deep end, too?

"Fine, a fucking hippo. This is so dumb." I grumbled quietly.

I put the car in drive and started us on our way home. I was looking all around on either side of the road searching for my sign and feeling like a dumbass until I heard in my mind, "You're not going to see it now. Forget about it for a while and just drive home." I did forget about it for the rest of the day. The whole experience had emotionally exhausted me, and life with a child under two had plenty of demands to keep me distracted.

Later that evening, I told my daughter to pick out a handful of books that she'd like me to read to her. While she wasn't speaking more than one word at a time here or there, she could understand me just fine. Her little arms were full of books that were spilling over as she toddled toward me. A huge smile spread over her face as she dumped them on the couch next to me. From the pile she handed me what turned out to be a picture book.

"Bea, there are no words in this book" I handed it back to her, "why don't you pick out one with words so that I can read it to you, okay?"

"No!" she shouted. That was a word she unfortunately knew very well. She shoved the book back in my face. "Dis," she said as she patted the book aggressively over and over.

"But Bea, it doesn't have any words in it, so I can't read it to you," I insisted. Still, she refused to grab a different book, so I agreed. She cozied up next to me, ready for me to show her the pictures. I turned the first page to see images of tropical birds. I pointed to each picture announcing the kind of bird that it was, but she interrupted me with her little hands and threw the book open to around the halfway mark. I swear I'd paged through picture books, including this one, with her hundreds of times at this point and had never seen the huge face that was grinning back at me from that book. Of course, it was the giant face of a hippo. I gasped and dropped the book on my lap. "No fuckin' way!" Bea startled and stared at me in question for a moment before she pointed at the page and started to giggle. I realize that it might sound like a silly story, but it was a moment for me when I just *knew* that this was in fact communication from something or someone much larger than myself. I nearly cried with relief, and I felt surrounded, supported, and profoundly loved in that moment.

Ask your spirit guides for a sign. Make it something that you don't usually come across. Most importantly, give it time, and stay open to the form that it might come to you in. I remember reading the book of a famous medium who suggested asking for a sign and waiting three days to two weeks for your sign. This is because sending signs requires energy from those on the other side, and apparently they have to arrange things just so. I figure that makes plenty of sense to me.

09
Command of Craft

The five Cs can get you a long way into your development as a medium, but how do you move to the level of truly feeling as though you have more of a command of your craft? How can you get to the point where you can give high-quality readings consistently? The Command of Craft C is about *how* you go about your mediumship development.

It's true that experience is sometimes the best teacher. That's why one part of Command of Craft focuses on regularly using your skills by giving readings consistently, and ideally, on a weekly basis. For example, when I began my mediumship journey, I decided that I would give 100 free readings. It was one of the best decisions that I made because inevitably it allowed me to experience many different sitters and different spirits, and it helped me to learn the language of Spirit. Some readings were really challenging or confusing until I began to notice a pattern about what certain spiritual impressions meant and how my mediumship works. I also discovered how many readings per week feel sustainable to me. At first, I gave two to three readings per week, but when people started referring others, it got busy fast. For a while, I was giving about five readings per week, and at one point my calendar had thirteen readings in a single week. I found out quickly that that was far too many readings for me and absolutely *not* sustainable long term. I now give about three readings a week on average, especially because I spend time each week teaching development circles and training workshops.

Command of Craft is also about strategic and organized learning. This means honing in on just one to two areas of improvement within your mediumship over a period of time. This doesn't mean that you don't partake in development circles or give readings consistently, encountering all kinds of exercises and experiences that will help you grow your skills. It does mean that you additionally choose only one to two areas of your practice that you feel you'd like to improve and work on each week to develop that area over a specified period of time.

To do this, I use my *What + 3 Hows* method. For example, let's say that I wanted to improve my ability to identify the cause of passing. I would begin by choosing that area of improvement as my *What*. Next, I decide my *3 Hows*. They will decide my approach to making this improvement. My first **How** is about <u>my way of improving this skill</u>, and it will be to study three new causes of passing each week. I will research them and learn about the symptoms. As I do this, I will create a clair symbol for each of the causes of passing that Spirit can communicate to me during a reading when the cause of passing applies.

My second **How** is <u>how often</u> I'll be studying three new causes of passing and creating clair symbols for each. For the second, it will be that I study three new causes each week.

The third **How** is about <u>how long</u> I'll continue this practice. For the third, it will be that I build up my knowledge and symbols about causes of passing for three months. To sum it up, for each specific area of your mediumship that you'd like to improve, you'll decide *What* that area is and *How* you'll improve it, *how often* and for *how long*.

Just think about how often you encounter a development circle or group where you simply come in each week doing the same thing. Or perhaps you're doing something different every week but without it feeling like it's organized in a strategic way so that your skills are building upon each other. The majority of groups and trainings that I've encountered go about mediumship in this way. It's not that you can't learn over time, but it simply isn't as effective as the Command of Craft approach and consistently working each of the 5 Cs of mediumship development. A combination of continuous practice using your skills *plus* focused, targeted steps toward improving your abilities to expand your mediumistic toolbox can help you progress more efficiently. Give it a try for the next month and see how you progress!

Command of Craft: Part One

Ex: I commit to giving two readings per week for the next month.

Your turn: I commit to giving _____ readings per week for the next month.

Command of Craft: Part Two

Ex:

What: Identify the cause of passing.

How: Research three causes of death and create clair symbols for each one that I can add to my Spirit Shorthand Journal.

How often: I'll research three causes of passing each week.

How long: I'll do this for three months and see how my ability to identify cause of passing improves.

Your turn:

What #1:

How:

How Often:

How Long:

What #2:

How:

How Often:

How Long:

10
Advanced Mediumship Skills

As you become more proficient in your practice of mediumship, Spirit will start to give you new challenges during your readings. Perhaps you were bringing through a single spirit during readings, and now multiples are showing up and making things a little more complex. You'll find yourself in situations where you might be working with other mediums and needing to link into the same Spirit. You may have clients who want to hear from a certain someone and not from the spirit who showed up. As soon as you think you've got this mediumship thing down, I promise that Spirit will leave you baffled by a new experience that requires new learning. It's one of the best things about this work. To help you anticipate some of the new experiences that might be coming your way, I'm sharing some additional tips that I, and many of my students, have found useful.

Presentation and Use of Language

You may not think of yourself as a speaker, presenter, or someone who is gifted linguistically, but if you want to be an excellent medium, you'll want to start. Watching a breathtaking reading is absolutely about the accurate evidence that comes through and the emotional and energetic healing that occurs. And, if you watch closely, you'll realize that an aspect of the best readings you've seen feature a medium who is verbally efficient and effective while also being a pleasant and compelling person to sit with. Am I telling you that you should create what feels like a broadway musical? No, but creating an energetic space for your sitter that is comfortable—a medium's equivalent of an inviting "bedside manner"—and not stumbling over your words and describing things in a way that is difficult to understand are very important skills to learn in order to give a high-quality reading.

In terms of *presentation*, there are a number of things to keep in mind:

1) Nobody cares how long the spirit has been hanging around you prior to your reading or what you were understanding about them beforehand.

I can't tell you how often I hear a medium begin a reading by saying something like, "So, I've had this older woman by my side the entire time and she has *not* left me alone! She was showing me x, y, z, and then started saying, a, b, c, and I was like whoa!" I have compassion because it often comes from nerves and a medium's need to show that they can communicate with Spirit and have been the entire time. The problem is it's boring to listen to and inefficient. It doesn't get straight to the point. Instead, I want to hear solid introductory evidence that can help identify who this spirit is right from the start. For example, "I've got a man with me that feels like a father. He suffered from alcoholism and passed tragically before his time. This man is here to speak with, or to get a message to, his daughter. He has apologies to make, most definitely..." Remember that you don't need to prove anything to anybody. You're here to find joy in doing your job and to do your absolute best to relay the message with accuracy.

2) No commentary or disclaimers please.

How would you feel if you sat down with a medium and the first thing out of their mouth was, "Okay, I have no idea if what I'm getting is something that you'll recognize, and I'm probably wrong, but...?" I can tell you right now that I'd ask for my money back. Again, I have compassion and empathy because I know that we take on a lot of pressure and responsibility as mediums, but as one of my most favorite activists in the world Billie Jean King says, "Pressure is a privilege," and it's our responsibility to manage it. As messengers, our job is to focus solely on what Spirit has to convey, not add commentary about how our day was or that we're getting over a cold so things might not be so clear, or that it's so wild what we're getting from Spirit right now, but oh well, we'll just say it even though it's probably wrong. I recommend recording yourself as you give a reading and listening for how often you put out a disclaimer or fill space with commentary that adds little to no value to the reading.

3) No need to repeat evidence multiple times to buy yourself time.

I know what you're thinking: *What if something the spirit is saying is super important and they want to emphasize it?* Sure, then say it twice, or say something like, "I can hear them saying 'It wasn't your fault' over and over again. They can't emphasize this enough." Don't be afraid to let a little silence in as that powerful moment settles and your sitter takes it in. It will get easier to move more efficiently through spiritual impressions as you continue to develop, so don't beat yourself up if you get a case of the repeats while you're stuck on one piece of information that you can't quite figure out. Eventually, though, you'll want to be more concise in your communication and move on. I tell my students to sort it out in their head and then speak clearly and with confidence out loud to your sitter. Spirit has much to say, and my favorite mentors were the first to tell me that Spirit never wastes a thought.

4) Be sensitive and compassionate when relaying emotional or delicate information.

Mediumship is not all rainbows and butterflies. Of course there is so much beauty, love, connection, and humor, but many of the readings that I give include death by suicide, abuse of all kinds, heavy grief, etc. As I previously mentioned in the section about mediumship ethics, remember to ask permission before diving headfirst into a sensitive topic with your sitter, especially if you are reading in a group setting where the sitter has less privacy. Once you do have permission to continue, be sensitive and compassionate in terms of how you put things. Many times a spirit will come through and apologize for abuse or infidelity. If I sense that this is too private, I may say, "They are apologizing for their lack of loyalty, if you can understand that" or "You went through some dark times with this person, and they are apologizing for how they hurt you. Do you understand?" I have other sitters who are happy for things to be said quite openly but even then, I'd still keep it on the classier side. For example, "They are referencing infidelity on their part and apologizing for how this hurt you" versus "They were an absolute perv who was balls-deep in anyone who breathed."

5) Break the habit of eyes-closed reading and connect with your sitter.

I'm not saying that you have to stare your sitter straight in the eyes or focus intently on them during a reading. It's absolutely fine if you don't look at your sitter for the entire reading. I begin my readings looking to the right because that is where all of my spiritual impressions come from. The problem is that when you close your eyes, you have little to no connection with your sitter. I've seen medium after medium with their eyes squeezed shut and slightly bent over looking like Quasimodo while their sitter is clearly confused by the information they've been bringing through for the past three minutes. It's easy to forget to check in with your sitter for validation or to get off on the wrong path without noticing. This is assuming that you're giving a reading where you can see your sitter. If you're giving a reading over the phone, this is obviously not applicable.

6) Don't be afraid to use humor.

Sometimes mediums can come across as only having that spiritual and sacred vibe. It can make anyone feel like laughter or joy in the presence of a passed spirit is inappropriate. I've found that Spirit loves for us to find joy and humor in their communication. Spirits often come through sharing memories that make us laugh. They joke, tease, and take great pleasure in bringing a smile to the sitter's face. Some of my favorite mediums allow humor to naturally come into their readings, and they are always the readings that move me the most. It reminds me of how I feel when I watch a great movie that runs the gamut of emotions and has me laughing, crying, and everything in between, and it's a therapeutic experience.

7) Don't ignore your audience.

I was in a mediumship class when I gave my first group reading, or platform reading, as some call it. I connected the spirit with a woman in the audience, and she validated what I brought through. My teacher let me know it was a job well done, but that it would have been much better if I hadn't ignored the rest of the people in the room. Include your audience. Mediumship isn't about putting on a show. It's about speaking to Spirit. But keep in mind that during a group reading, every person came to feel more connection and love. They may not be the sitter who is connected to the spirit coming through, but there's something in the spirit's message for all of us if we're listening and truly open. I've watched some of the best mediums onstage, and while they are focused primarily on their connection with Spirit and the sitter they are working with, they bring the audience in and never forget to look around the room at the other faces who are watching this conversation play out.

Once I gave a reading for a group of doulas that were celebrating a birthday. Several of the people attending received readings, but not every person. As I was bringing through the deceased father of one of the women there, I noticed that the woman sitting behind her was sobbing and doing her best to stifle a full-on ugly cry session. I paused for just a moment and looked over to her, "Wait? Why are *you* crying?" I asked with lots of love and humor. The room erupted with laughter, and that moment brought incredible connection and levity to every person watching. The woman replied to me, "I can't help it, it's just so beautiful!" and by then she had moved on to craughing, which is crying and laughing at the same time.

When it comes to the *use of language*, here's what I aim for and how I improve my use of language: The bottom line is that you want to be efficient, compelling, and clear. That means that when you watch a reading, you don't want to feel like you're working to figure out what the medium means when they speak. In a class of mine, I had a student working mediumistically and describing the outdoor space around the house that the spirit had lived in before passing. She was going back and forth between hearing crunching leaves, smelling pine trees, and describing soap. I could tell she was managing many different impressions but hadn't really pieced them all together in a way that was clear. When she asked her sitter if the information she was bringing through made sense, her sitter's face looked incredibly confused and she responded, "I'm not really sure what you're describing. Can you repeat that?" When things aren't clear and efficient, they are rarely compelling, if ever. Everyone watching starts to squirm a little in their seats because we're all waiting for those juicy moments of validation that bring up feelings in us. As I linked into the spirit, I could tell she had been a real woman of nature. If I was to bring across the evidence my student was sorting through, I'd say, "This woman was a lover of nature. There were woods behind her house and lots of leaves in the fall. She wasn't a perfume type of person. Her soaps smelled natural, like pine trees." We want to make ourselves clear and to the point so our sitter can easily respond, and our audience—if we're reading for a group—is right there with us.

Here is a simple list of things you can do to improve your use of language:

- Watch great speakers who you view as compelling to listen to.
- Read or listen to books that include descriptive depictions of things, people, places, and feelings.
- Look up every word that you come across and don't know the meaning of. Practice using it in context.
- Practice describing your own feelings, appearance, or character out loud as if you're writing a book.

Working with More Than One Spirit

When I was first developing my skills, I brought through one spirit during most of my readings, but it wasn't long before two or more spirits at a time started showing up. It makes sense. A lot of people have many passed loved ones with things to say. Nowadays I'm aware of multiple spirits in the majority of my readings. The time is rarely divided equally between them, but depending on the length of the reading, I might be able to bring through a significant message from two to four passed loved ones. Other times there's a main communicator who takes priority and has a lot to say, and we only have time for quick hellos from the rest, if that. In order to manage my readings in an organized way, I use four practices to help identify when multiple spirits are present.

1) Begin with the power of intention.

It's easy to forget just how powerful intentions are. Spirit is very much aware of our intentions, and setting them before we begin a reading does a world of good. If you'd like to bring through just one spirit, set that intention. If you'd like to bring through more than one spirit, set that intention. In the case of multiples, intend as well that it's clear to you who is who, and which evidence goes with which spirit. As I've previously shared, I say a short prayer before I begin my readings, and the part that helps me keep spirits straight sounds like this: "Help me bring through a passed loved one or loved ones who are recognizable and fantastic spirit communicators who are easy for me to understand."

2) Notice who's present.

Early on, I would begin a reading by waiting to become aware of the energy of a single passed spirit. Now when I begin my readings, I begin similarly, but I additionally focus on expanding my energy and taking a moment to clairvoyantly "look around." The best way for me to describe this is that it's as if I see spirits off to my right side in my peripheral vision. When there is more than one present, they look a little like separate silhouettes to me clairvoyantly in my mind's eye. I also feel their individual energies clairsentiently.

At this point, I don't need to necessarily know exactly who each spirit is, although I often have a sense. My priority is to notice which spirit is stepping forward to blend with me. Once you feel the presence of that spirit, you can begin identifying them and bringing through evidence. However, here is another thing to *notice*! Once you begin with that spirit, you may initially get yeses, but if you then start getting nos or a mixture of both from the start, there's a good chance that you're picking up evidence from more than one spirit and only attributing that evidence to the one you've begun bringing through. A mixture of yeses and nos or a sudden switch from "yes" to "no" can often be a sign of multiple spirits. As soon as this happens, I make an energetic shift that to me feels like looking *behind* the main spirit that I'm aware of. Another way of saying it is that I expand my awareness further out beyond just the spirit that I've been channeling. You may have to play with this in the moment to see how you sense multiple spirits.

If you have trouble being able to tell when there's more than one spirit, you can always ask your sitter, "Does *some* of the evidence that I'm bringing through apply to more than just one passed loved one?" They'll usually respond with "yes" and let you know that they first thought it was one person and now are wondering if it is someone else.

3) Ask the spirit for evidence that differentiates them.

At this point, there may be an easy fix to get you back on track with one spirit at a time. I ask the spirit I began channeling to give me evidence that will differentiate them from any other passed spirit, and then I relax into receiving that next spiritual impression. Maybe they share with you that they were married or divorced or the side of the family they were on. They could share whether they were a smoker or a hobby that they absolutely loved. These are just examples of what might be true about one passed spirit but not the other that your sitter was wondering about. Best case scenario is that you bring through more evidence that matches up with just one spirit and that your sitter now understands who is speaking to them. You've done what we call "anchoring the link," and you can continue on. If you keep getting nos or a mixture of yeses and nos, you'll have to take a different approach.

4) Hold your boundary and ask for one at a time.

If you still find yourself with two spirits who seem to be vying for the spotlight, which can happen, since spirits have needs too, you'll have to lay down your boundary—and *mean* it—that you only work with one spirit at a time. Within my mind, I say, "I will not work with more than one of you at a time. Please line up. Will the main communicator please step forward?" There have been times when I have to say this more than once, but it usually works out. After I've asked for the main communicator to step forward, I feel into their presence to make sure I understand who I'm working with and can anchor the link. Then I'm finally ready to continue with that spirit. It can also be helpful to recap any "yes" evidence that is associated with the spirit who has stepped forward in order to strengthen the link with that spirit and build the energy as you move forward with the reading.

What To Do When Your Evidence Matches for a Living Person

Every once in a while, we might find ourselves bringing through evidence that our sitter tells us matches up to a living person. What do we do then? First, if you're earlier on in your development and you find this happening to you more often, don't panic. Mediums in the earlier stages of development can be unaware of when they may be dropping into the psychic vibration. Remember that the psychic vibration is lower than the mediumistic vibration. This often corrects over time as you build up your energetic stamina, but as I mentioned early on, this is why it is so important to be able to distinguish between the two. In this case, it may be helpful to ask your clients before the reading to let you know if the evidence you bring through matches up with a living person.

Once you're aware that your evidence is for a living person, you'll want to check in to see if you are reading psychically or mediumistically. If you feel that you are at a mediumistic vibration, or even if you don't feel that, you'll want to make that same energetic shift that I shared with you in the case of multiple spirits. For me, it's as if I'm looking behind the living person that I'm sensing in the same way that I look behind a spirit to see if there is more than one spirit present. In other words, I'm expanding my awareness beyond what I've been initially receiving.

I remember doing a reading with a friend of mine early on in my development. I was getting really strong spiritual impressions about a man and describing the evidence to her. She told me that this matched up perfectly with her living ex-boyfriend who she had recently broken up with. At that time I wasn't aware of how to handle the situation, so we decided to continue on for a bit. Evidence about him just kept coming, and I felt that I was meant to tell her things about healing from the breakup. Because I thought that I wasn't connecting to a spirit, we instead decided to end the reading.

Months later when she was visiting me in my home, and after I had had a mentor who explained this concept to me, we remembered the reading. I instantly became aware of her ex-boyfriend's grandparents on his mother's side and asked my friend if they were deceased. She said they were. I said that I felt they had been very close to him and that his grandfather had passed from a heart attack. She confirmed that this was true and that her ex-boyfriend had witnessed the heart attack when he was young. He had been heartbroken after losing his grandparents. His grandmother was communicating this to me and had been the spirit that was bringing through the information about him during my friend's reading. She was looking to give my friend understanding about the breakup and peace as she moved forward. If I had known at that time to look beyond the evidence I was getting about her ex-boyfriend, I would have become aware of his grandparents. His grandmother was the main communicator, and she felt familiar to me when I made the connection months later.

Controlling Who Comes Through Versus Allowing Whoever Comes

My preference when I work professionally is to allow whoever comes. This means that I trust that the spirit who comes through and the message that they give will be the most helpful and healing to my sitter. In other words, I don't ask my sitter who they want to hear from. I do share with them that I believe Spirit has a much better perspective than we do here on earth and that this is why I leave it up to Spirit. I also feel that it's an even more powerful experience for my sitter when the person they want to hear from comes through without me knowing who that person is. Ninety-nine percent of the time, I find that the person who comes through *is* the person who my sitter wants to hear from. With this approach, while my sitters usually get what they want, they just about always get what they need.

Other mediums work by asking their sitter who they want to hear from at the start of the reading. They may also ask for a first name. There's nothing wrong or unethical with this. Both ways can work.

At a training I attended, our instructor paired us up and had us give two readings to our partner. One was a reading where we allowed whoever wanted to come through to do so. The next was a reading where our sitter asked us to bring through someone specific.

As I conducted both readings back to back, I realized there wasn't much of a difference between the two ways of working. In both cases, you use the power of intention and become aware of the spirit that is stepping forward. As you develop your skills, you can see what works best for you. I continue to favor allowing whoever comes.

The most powerful part of evidential mediumship is bringing through spirits and evidence that we have no prior knowledge of and that can be validated. In light of that, allowing whoever comes feels more in alignment for me. That being said, I received a reading from a tutor at a residential mediumship study program. She first brought through a spirit who wasn't recognizable to me. After a few minutes, she ended that attempt and asked me who I wanted to hear from. I told her I wanted to hear from my grandfather on my father's side. She began again but started bringing through my grandfather on my mother's side. On her third attempt, she was able to bring through the person I wanted to hear from. While I was a little surprised that it took three attempts, I was glad that she had asked me who I wanted to hear from. It saved time and energy, and it was a very powerful experience for me.

Photo Readings

I happen to love photo readings even though I find them to be difficult. A photo reading is one of the most challenging mediumistic practices you can do. Think about it: You have no one sitting in front of you to validate your evidence. You may start picking up all kinds of information, but without that validation, it's easy to get off on the wrong track, especially if you haven't set a strong intention.

Photo readings are a powerful exercise for these reasons:

1) Photo readings retain the pressure that comes with mediumship, but not the urgency.

We all feel pressure when we read. Overcoming that pressure is a skill that you must hone as a medium. In a photo reading, you'll likely still feel that pressure to be accurate, but you won't feel that same urgency that we do when a live sitter is in front of us. When we do read for someone who is present, it can be easy to rush ourselves and feel that we need to present them with lots of evidence, and quickly. Being able to slow down and focus in as we read can help us gain the courage and confidence to read at our own pace.

2) Photo readings don't allow you to rely on your sitter too much or accidentally cold read them—which is unethical.

I've mentioned that often in classes, I'll tell my students to wait to give feedback until the end of the reading or have my students read with their sitter's video off. Photo readings are an even more extreme version of that. Because there is no feedback whatsoever, you train yourself to focus more on your connection with Spirit than on your sitter, which is how it should be. If you haven't heard of "cold reading," it's an unethical practice where a medium essentially reads the body language of their sitter and claims to have a spiritual connection. This is obviously fraudulent. If you rely too much on your sitter and their responses, you may start to react to their reactions instead of connecting more deeply with Spirit.

3) Photo readings give you time to interview the spirit or ask questions.

While some mediums work by asking the spirit questions throughout the reading, others are more Spirit-lead. I am a Spirit-lead medium. That means that I follow the spirit's lead during a reading. For me, the information comes so quickly that I don't usually have time to ask questions. In a photo reading, regardless of how you work, you have more spacious time to practice asking a spirit questions.

4) Photo readings give you time to focus on evidence that you don't always get and clairs that you don't always use.

Another benefit of having more space in a photo reading, since no one is actually sitting with you, is feeling more comfortable playing with more of your less dominant clairs. Perhaps you don't smell or taste as often in a reading and you want to play with those clairs. Perhaps you want to dive into the cause of passing and take more time to receive the details. Photo readings are a great time to expand the way you work and therefore expand your skills overall.

How To Begin a Photo Reading

Many mediums will teach you to begin a photo reading by looking into the spirit's eyes. This can start the connection and invite spiritual impressions. I've had students for whom this works extremely well. For others, any details about the picture may make them feel like they are making assumptions or being thrown off. I begin my photo readings by looking into the spirit's eyes, but then I "wash my mind" of the picture and use the power of intention to connect with the spirit in the photo.

Why do I do it this way? The brain is a powerful processing machine. It makes all kinds of assumptions about what it sees in a matter of seconds. Most of these assumptions are unconscious and are based upon our own frame of reference. When I take that time to look into the eyes of the spirit person in the photo, I'm conscious of intending to feel into them clairsentiently versus taking in every detail visually.

However you choose to connect with the spirit person in a photo, here are three ways to go about it:

1) You might focus on them quickly and then connect with their spirit for just ten minutes to see what spiritual impressions you receive.

For many, not giving themselves an assignment of receiving specific evidence—at least as they begin—can help to create a strong connection and allow the experience to flow.

2) You can create a list of evidence you'd like to receive and fill out the answer you get for each one.

This is a little more challenging, but it can help you to develop the power of focus during a reading. Just remember that not all spirits communicate in the same way or answer every question that we ask.

3) You could go for a full-blown reading where you record yourself bringing the spirit through and then give it back to the sitter and have them tell you what was accurate.

After you've practiced a few photo readings, this can be a great way to go. There are foundations, such as the Windbridge Research Center, that conduct blind testing where the medium has no information about the passed spirit or the sitter. Photo readings are a great way to prepare for this kind of experience.

Where to Get Photos

I have a spiritual women's group I attend, and I asked those who were interested to give me pictures of passed loved ones so I could practice photo readings. I created a list of questions that I asked them to answer about the person in their photo. I didn't look at the answers until after I did the photo reading so that I could check how accurate I was. I then passed on messages to my friends from these passed loved ones.

When I teach photo readings, I ask past clients that I've read for if I can use a photo of their passed loved one. I let them know it's for a class reading. I then pass on relevant information and messages that have come through from my students after the exercise.

Don't panic if you bomb a photo reading. It is an advanced exercise. I've participated in many exercises only to flunk some of them and then go on to give an incredible mediumistic reading. Have fun, and remember that exercises are meant to help you flex your mediumistic muscles and build your spiritual skills. Don't forget that after a photo reading, a reading with a live person will feel much easier!

Linking In/Sharing a Contact

Being able to link in or share a contact is a wonderful skill to develop in your mediumship practice. When you're linking in, you're connecting to the same spirit as a fellow medium. For example, let's say I've given my students the task of quickly identifying the spirit and getting specific about the role a spirit plays to the sitter. I go to observe a student of mine who is bringing through a woman who died before her time from a tragic illness. My student can sense that this passing happened somewhat suddenly and swiftly, but is having trouble identifying the relationship this spirit had to the sitter. I link into this same spirit that my student is bringing through, and I can feel that this spirit woman was very maternal in her role and a part of the immediate family of my sitter. I hear "mom," and when I ask how she passed, I'm taken to the head, and I hear "tumor." I'm now able to direct my student toward certain pieces of evidence to help her focus her mind in the areas that will reveal the role that the spirit played to the sitter.

When it comes to linking in and sharing a contact, I'm sure you won't be surprised that, once again, the power of intention is extremely useful. I tell my students when they are linking in that if the power of intention doesn't naturally bring them awareness of the same spirit of their partnering medium, then they should expand their energetic fields into their partnering medium's energetic field, the same way you would if you were going to work psychically. From there, you may more easily link into the same spirit. It is not nearly as complicated as you might think and essentially not any different than setting an intention about linking into a specific spirit were a sitter to ask you to contact a certain passed loved one of theirs. When my students are practicing this, I tell them to let one medium begin the reading by anchoring the link and the second medium to then link into the spirit in the ways I previously shared.

When You Might Share a Contact and Link In

Sharing a contact can be so much fun! There are a few different situations where you might link in with a fellow medium. I have my students link into the same spirit during class. I do this when we have an uneven number of students in class. When we divide up to do practice readings, I have two students read one student, and I ask them to share a contact. In my intermediate and advanced classes, I teach linking in as a skill. While linking in isn't as advanced as you might think, I've found that many of my beginner students get distracted or lose confidence when they hear other students sharing evidence that they aren't aware of. Sometimes they may also get nervous if they feel they are aware of a different spirit than the one that they are meaning to link into. These are normal challenges, but just like in any situation where you are giving a reading, stay focused on your own connection to the spirit. This spirit will work off of your frame of reference, and this is often why you will expand the body of evidence that is being given and it will not always be evidence that others are aware of.

You might also need to be able to use the skill of linking in when you work with another medium to run a workshop or a training or to do a group reading or a reading from the stage. I was giving a reading with another medium, and this partnering medium started to bring through the father of our sitter. I could sense that her relationship with her father had been tumultuous. He had left the family in a dire financial situation after a messy divorce with her mother. My partnering medium started to describe the relationship between the sitter and her father in spirit as harmonious. I believed she was attributing valid evidence about the sitter's grandfather on her mother's side and mother to her father in spirit. When nos started coming, my partnering medium had me jump in, and I was able to bring through evidence about the father that the sitter understood and confirmed. I passed it back to my partnering medium, who was able to accurately describe the relationship between the sitter and her mother.

While I mentioned that beginner mediums who hear evidence they weren't aware of from a partnering medium can sometimes feel intimidated or lose confidence, the beauty of linking in is that you often do bring different aspects of the spirit person through in a way that brings complexity and depth to the reading. I was working with another medium who was fantastic with detailed evidence. He and I were bringing through the passed mother of a man. My partner was great with bringing through the details about her passing and how the house was set up for hospice care. When he handed it off to me, I was able to give him a crucial message from his mother that hit home and brought him to tears. It was a message that he really needed to hear from her. Between the two of us as mediums, we were able to give a beautiful reading that was incredibly impactful for our sitter.

If you have any aspirations for teaching mediumship, linking in is crucial and something you must be able to do. Your ability to link into a spirit can help provide additional context to your student when they feel stuck and direct them to evidence and messages that have more depth when they are reading, bringing in more complexity to their readings.

I facilitate a reading assessment workshop where mediums get to come and read in a group setting to get real-time coaching plus feedback after the reading that goes deeply into deconstructing their mediumship mechanics. In order to coach my students during their observed reading when needed and to give them constructive and useful feedback after their reading about what was going on and working well, and about what could be improved, I have to be able to link in.

Students also come to me when they've been through a tricky reading or mediumship experience between classes and they want to sort out what happened. I can usually link in afterward and get insight for them so we can break down what happened and how to handle a similar situation in the future. Linking in is a must even to be able to simply help a student along during practice readings in class, let them know they've got multiple spirits or that they're interpreting evidence in a way that is not accurate, etc. Ultimately, you've got to be able to understand what's happening during your student's readings to give them constructive and effective feedback. I've been in far too many circles where the instructor only observes and doesn't break down a reading to help a student recognize what they excelled at and what they have the opportunity to expand upon.

When You Shouldn't Link In

It is proper mediumship etiquette *not* to link into the spirit that another medium is working with if you are not in agreement about sharing the contact, not teaching, or an observer in any other situation. Linking into the spirit of another medium can dilute the energy and make it more difficult for the medium to connect, so please do not do it unless you are in one of the situations I described above. Many mediums like to test out their skills here or there without realizing that it's an absolute nuisance to the medium who is working. They may not have been told it's not good etiquette.

A mentor of mine told me that she was giving readings from the stage, and nothing was landing. She was having a difficult time connecting. She took a minute to consult with her guides about what might be happening. She said she was told by them that the audience was full of mediums who were trying to connect with her contact. She addressed the audience and asked for any mediums to please stop trying to connect during the reading. After that, everything went smoothly.

Spiritual Assessments

What is a spiritual assessment? A spiritual assessment is an assessment of where you are with your spiritual abilities as a medium, intuitive, or both. The main purpose of it is to give a spiritual practitioner clarity, understanding, and validation about how their gifts work and what challenges or opportunities they might encounter and insight into their unfolding path. When I give spiritual assessments, I often become aware of dominant clairs that practitioners use, experiences they have had and are having with Spirit, aspects of their personal life that tie into their development as a spiritual practitioner, where they feel challenged, what kind of spiritual work they might be called to, and more. I recommend getting a spiritual assessment from someone who is highly regarded as a mentor and advanced as a spiritual practitioner themselves.

How Are Spiritual Assessments Run?

There isn't necessarily a right or wrong way to give a spiritual assessment, but it should definitely provide clarity, validation, and encouragement to someone who is seeking to develop their spiritual abilities. When I give assessments, I break the reading into two parts. During the first part, I work intuitively to become aware of where you are on your spiritual path, what brought you there, what you're currently doing to strengthen your skills, many of the above-mentioned aspects, etc. During the second part of the reading, I work mediumistically with your spirit team to give you any necessary or helpful messages and guidance from them. I love giving spiritual assessments because they are all so unique to each person. I gave an assessment to a student once, and it came to me that he had always felt somewhat of an outsider among others. Communication with others didn't always come easily or make sense, and I understood that when he entered into relationships openly and with a strong intent to deeply connect, he often felt other people's discomfort at his kind and direct nature. He is also one of my students who primarily worked claircognizantly when he came to me, and this was reflected in the telepathic relationship that he had with his mother when she was alive. When I went to connect with his spirit team, they told me that he had incarnated on earth from somewhere else in the cosmos and that human's ways of being could often feel foreign to him.

"Are you telling me that I'm an alien?" he asked.

"I think so?" I felt strange saying it out loud. I can't tell you that I have much more understanding than that because it sounded insane to me, but the wildest thing is that it resonated deeply with him. We still joke in my mediumship classes now that he is the resident alien.

The Benefits of a Spiritual Assessment

Assessments can be incredibly helpful, especially in terms of giving you validation as a spiritual practitioner. Work with Spirit can feel so elusive, and having someone else understand what your journey has been like can offer so much encouragement and clarity. Often when I've received a spiritual assessment, the medium has been able to affirm things that I've been sensing myself, like the main spirit guides I've been working with, the ways that I excel as a medium, and the challenges I've been facing and how to overcome them.

My first-ever spiritual assessment was chock-full of benefits! Not only did it strongly affirm things that I'd been seeing and hearing about my path and future as a medium, but in addition, the medium told me to do something that she said she'd never told anyone to do. She said, "You need to start a YouTube channel ASAP. You're gonna need it. People are going to want to see your work so that they can give you certain invitations and opportunities to read or speak on stages." This happened within the first three months of my mediumship journey and completely altered my path in the best way, making it possible for me to work professionally just seven months into my journey. I've had other spiritual assessments since. Some have been much more helpful than others. One affirmed for me that one of my paths is the path of the teacher, which eased me into beginning my own development circles and training workshops.

When to Get a Spiritual Assessment

When you feel that you are ready for clarity, encouragement, and some direction and guidance about your mediumistic and intuitive gifts, it's a great time to receive a spiritual assessment from a medium that you trust and respect. Just keep in mind that if you're just getting started on your journey, or even if you're a ways in, you might be highly sensitive to the information and guidance that you receive. If for any reason it doesn't resonate with you, take it with a grain of salt. No one knows you better than you do, and no one ultimately knows your mediumship better than you, either, even if you're just at the beginning of your unfoldment. Ultimately, a spiritual assessment should be an encouraging and positive experience that gives you clarity and inspiration. Always make sure that you ignore anyone who tries to put limits on you or mislead you by telling you what *isn't* possible for you.

When to Give a Spiritual Assessment

I don't recommend jumping into giving spiritual assessments until you feel you are at a certain level of proficiency with your own spiritual abilities. That means that you should feel highly skilled in both your intuitive and mediumistic abilities. You should also be able to tell the difference between working psychically and mediumistically. This is important because you'll have to work psychically to look into someone's spiritual file within their energetic field, and you'll have to work mediumistically to connect with their spirit team. The guidelines I follow are the same as moving into becoming a teacher or mentor. This may sound harsh, and I don't know about you, but personally, I don't want advice, guidance, or "clarity" unless it's of the highest quality and from someone who has at least a command of their craft at the level I do.

That being said, so many of us struggle with confidence and undervalue our skills, so don't wait to give them if you've got the proof that your connection is accurate and you're consistently working at an advanced level. You'll definitely find, once you're ready, that other aspiring mediums will come looking for this kind of guidance and that it can be a powerful thing to add to your repertoire of services.

11
Mediumship Maintenance and Sustainability + Best Practices

There's a honeymoon stage that manifests as a super-high as you're coming into your gifts. This honeymoon stage extends itself for a while as you begin giving readings and blowing your own mind with the evidence that comes through. As with anything, you haven't touched reality yet when you're in this phase. Until you land from the honeymoon and come down from the high, you have no idea what mediumship maintenance and sustainability looks and feels like for the long term.

I often feel gratitude that I entered into mediumship in my late thirties. From what I've seen, older mediums tend to have a better chance of weathering the ups and downs of mediumship simply due to having had a longer life experience. Instead of what might feel like mountain tops and valleys, we have a higher likelihood of traveling over hills, into ditches, and across plains.

Luckily for me, the mediums I started following were younger mediums. Unfortunately, I saw a lot of examples and heard a lot of stories of major burnout and sometimes even physical illness. Going into mediumship, I was much more cautious and vigilant than I would have been in my twenties or even early thirties about how often I choose to read. I also tried to be introspective about how my body was responding to this work. I will say that even with those precautions, I ran into some curveballs and found myself pulling back just a bit from the number of one-on-one readings I give regularly and expanding my work in other complimentary ways that also bring me joy and help me to continue developing my skills.

We'll continue to dive into mediumship maintenance, but first, let me share the three different ways that I evaluate whether or not my work as a medium is truly sustainable. The only caveat is that sometimes as you're growing skills or creating something new, you go through chapters that are more or less sustainable long-term but serve a powerful purpose for the short term.

Emotionally and Energetically Sustainable

Remember when I pointed out that most mediums are pretty strong empaths? This means that working as a medium can affect us emotionally. We are working with clients regularly who are grieving their passed loved ones and who emote during readings. I would say in 90% or more of my readings, my sitters feel large emotions and shed tears. While I'm an empathetic person, I do have healthy emotional boundaries that are strong. This allows me to be an empath and feel deeply but to avoid taking on other people's emotions as my own. Where you are with your ability to hold space for others and handle emotions, whether they are yours or others', can affect how often you use your gifts mediumistically. In addition to emotional capacity and health, we also have to take into consideration our energetic capacity. I had a teacher who shared with me that different people have not just different levels of energy, but also different kinds of energy. While I'm no expert in the different types of energy we have as humans, I'm sure all of us can think of a person we know who seems like an energizer bunny—they just keep going. I've always been a high-energy person myself, but I'm no energizer bunny. I've gone through times in my life where I've needed lots of rest, like pregnancy, or have had heavy bouts of anxiety. These times have not afforded me the energy to give as many readings. For me, there's nothing worse than going into a reading feeling tired or exhausted. While I can usually pull it off, it's not my favorite way to work.

I find that the most important advice I take myself and give to my clients is to pay attention to how you feel emotionally and energetically after you work. Not just after a single reading, but after an entire week of work or a large group reading. If you don't feel like you've figured out what's emotionally and energetically sustainable for you yet, it would be wise to take a moment to really pay attention to your body after you work and then write down your experience. It's easy to feel lots of excitement when it goes well, but you'll have to come down from that excitement eventually.

I remember watching a famous medium who never seemed to quit and gave the most remarkable readings. I said to myself, "It would be nice to have that much energy and never feel it, but good for them." Then I found out from another medium that she'd spoken to a family member of theirs and discovered that after group readings, they suffer from horrible headaches and often get sick to the point of vomiting! I've never had that experience, but I haven't worked at the level of this famous medium. If I'm honest, it made me feel a lot better to know that everyone is human and that this work *does* affect us, so we have to know what that effect is and learn to take great care of ourselves so it can remain enjoyable and sustainable. I have no intention of changing my profession ever again, so I'm committed to working in a way that keeps me loving it for a lifetime. Once you feel like you've got a handle on this aspect of sustainability, you'll be able to say with more confidence how often you like to use your gifts.

Emotional and energetic sustainability exercise:

Create a journal for at least the next week. Each time after you use your gifts, take three minutes to tune into your body and see where you're at. Document how you feel emotionally and energetically. Make sure to also pay attention to these details the day, or days, after you work to see if there is a delayed effect.

Creative Sustainability and Fulfillment

One of the things I love so much about mediumship and spiritual work is that there are so many unknowns and uncertainties! Sure, this can be a pain at times when you feel baffled by your work, but it also means that there is no end to the adventure that comes along with the job. I don't find myself getting bored, because I know there are so many ways to use my gifts. I *can* tell you that if I only gave one-on-one readings, I'd be tired, bored, and ready to move on after a few years. As a highly creative person, one-on-one readings are wonderful, and I feel constantly challenged to do better, but I also get excited about expanding my work and knowledge. I love taking classes, teaching classes, delving deeper into meditation, giving spiritual assessments, creating spiritual decks, and creating content that people can learn from, like my YouTube videos or this book. I look forward to reading from a stage more often for large crowds, giving readings to inmates, fundraising through this work for causes I believe in, and so much more. After my first year working as a medium, I was thrilled about all of these options and knew that I'd be delving into each of them when the time was right.

Creative sustainability and fulfillment exercise:

Think about what has brought you the most creative fulfillment in your life.

1. What patterns have you noticed about yourself in terms of feeling fulfilled long-term when it comes to your work or purpose?
2. What ideas and dreams do *you* have for yourself as a medium when it comes to different ways to use your gifts?

Financially Sustainable

Perhaps you have no intention of working professionally as a medium. No problem! If you do want to work professionally, then financial sustainability is something you'll most definitely have to take into consideration. Unless you're a famous medium who charges a pretty high price for a reading and serves people who will invest at that level, like celebrities, I don't know any mediums who have a fully financially sustainable business by only giving private readings. Even if you are in that boat, you'd be unlikely to tick our first two boxes: emotionally and energetically sustainable and creative sustainability and fulfillment.

There are three mistakes I see mediums make who want to create a living today. First, most mediums try to scale and profit by offering more one-on-one readings (or one-on-one offers of any kind that have them trading dollars for hours). Second, they get sucked into the low-wealth consciousness of the mediumship industry and feel anxiety about even *thinking* of charging money for their services even though they have every right to, just like in any other profession. And third, they fail to create a business model that provides the pathway to profitability. After making the first mistake, it's painful to realize that you need a proper ratio of working *in* your business versus *on* your business. A client of mine said to me, "I have terrible boundaries, and I'm not a planner or a strategic person. I just squeeze in more and more private readings, and I never have time to think about how I can branch out and do this differently."

Along with creative sustainability and fulfillment, financial sustainability for a medium is about branching out and using your gifts in even a small handful of different ways that allow you to help more people than simply trading dollars for hours. Group readings and teaching are two examples of this. In my own business, I have two offers that have me trading dollars for hours, private readings and spiritual assessments. Besides those two offers, all of my others allow me to work with many people at once: my mediumship development circles, mediumship training courses, mediumship business course, group readings, and all of the different forms of content that I create that are available to many and lead to my programs for those who are interested. If you're a medium looking to make a living from your work and you need step-by-step guidance, check out my next book, *The Profitable Spiritual Medium: How to make 6 figures and beyond talking to dead people.*

Financial sustainability exercise:

Take some time to sit and reflect on whether or not you feel called to mediumship as a profession. If you are at a point in your journey where you want to envision making a living as a medium, answer these questions.

1. Do you feel ready to start charging for your services? Why or why not?
2. What are three services you'd like to offer that use your gifts mediumistically? *Make sure at least one of them serves many instead of trading dollars for hours.*

3. What yearly income would you need to create to make mediumship sustainable for you in all three ways that've been discussed in this book? *Work backward to find out how many of each offer you'd need to sell and then subtract your expenses.*

Grounding and Protecting Your Energy

Just about every medium you meet will tell you that they have different beliefs around the need to ground, center, protect their energy, and more. Some mediums believe that it is vital, and the responsible thing to do, to protect yourself from dark energies and entities, etc. While I don't deny that dark energies or entities may very well exist—after all, there is good and evil here on earth, so wouldn't it make sense that those energetic polarities may also be present in another dimension as well—I have little worry that they will interfere with me and my work.

In my experience as an incarnated person and as a medium, I've found that spirits are a lot like living people when it comes to boundaries. If you are clear within yourself and with them about what you're available for and *not* available for, they will generally observe those boundaries. I hear many mediums complain about other people and spirits not observing their boundaries. This *can* absolutely be the reality; however, usually I see this happen when the person laying down the boundaries hasn't really fully taken ownership of those boundaries. Think for a moment about an experience you've had with someone who laid out a boundary for you and *meant* it. You could feel the truth in their boundary and that it was not something that was going to budge. Now think about a boundary that was laid out by someone, yet you felt their wavering conviction. Those are two different experiences that get very different results.

When I'm working with Spirit, I can feel my non-negotiable and unwavering conviction that states to Spirit that I am only available to work with spirits that come to me with the intention of honest communication with their living loved ones and that will provide the most healing possible. As I share with you my practices for grounding, centering, intention, and protecting your energy, I encourage you to be introspective about your own belief systems and spiritual boundaries. You may resonate with my practices or find that you need more or less to feel comfortable and safe working as a medium.

Grounding

To work mediumistically and connect with Spirit, we must elevate our vibration as Spirit temporarily lowers theirs so that we can meet in the middle. I often feel the difference in my body as I speak to spirits, and there can be a bit of a high that follows. Grounding is an important aspect to practice before and after readings to keep your head in reality. I've spoken with plenty of spiritual practitioners who have their heads so high up in the clouds that it's difficult to have a conversation with them. It's a shame, too, because the people who need this work the most are more likely to venture into it if they feel they're connecting with someone who feels resonant and relatable to them.

My grounding practice is simple and quick. As I sit to connect with Spirit, the first thing I imagine in my mind's eye is my root chakra at the base of my spine anchoring me firmly into my seat. This gives me confidence and assurance that I'm in control of my body and secure. This takes me all of ten seconds, so there's no need to make a production out of it. Just like boundaries, grounding and protecting your energy requires you to trust yourself and your own commitment to your convictions. When my reading is over, I imagine the same thing. If I feel like I need something extra, exercising, going for a walk, or getting a massage can be extremely helpful to get me back in my body.

Grounding exercise:

Before you sit down to connect to Spirit, focus first on your breath, observing it for three breath cycles. With every exhale, let your shoulders drop. As you inhale, bring your attention to your root chakra at the base of your spine. Feel your root chakra light up and strongly intend that it helps to ground you to the earth. You can play with imagining roots extending from your body down into the earth, or simply focus on feeling a subtle but firm tug that lets you know you're grounded. See what works for you and sit for a few minutes, knowing you are grounded and secure.

Protecting Your Energy

Remember that working as a medium requires you to work with your own energy and the energy of Spirit. It's such an intangible and sometimes elusive thing for so many of us, and yet we all feel the effects in one way or another. Consider too that many mediums are hardcore empaths. This means they strongly feel the energy of others and even tend to take it on as their own, for better or worse. When I begin my readings, after I quickly ground myself, I imagine a second image in my mind's eye that looks like a clear, large bubble surrounding my energetic field, about five feet out from where I am sitting. This bubble is a barrier that protects my energy from the energy of my sitter and from the energy of Spirit. But it's not just about having this barrier in place. It's also about strengthening your ability to tell the difference between what's yours and what's not yours. I can't tell you how many mediums struggle during readings because they are too affected by the energy of their sitter or they've taken on the emotions being communicated by the spirit so fully that they can't separate themselves. Indeed, the energy of our sitter can be a real bitch to deal with at times. You might get a serious skeptic, a Chatty Cathy, a kind person with a resting bitch face, and more. Regardless, mediumship isn't just about having the ability to speak to Spirit; it's also about keeping your nerve and being able to prioritize and focus on your communication with Spirit above all else, with the confidence that you're operating as a clear channel. I've had this conversation with my students continuously, reminding them to ask themselves a simple question when they feel they're being swept into the energy of someone or something else's: "What's mine? Okay, what's not mine?" Just this simple question trains you to practice becoming aware of that empathic tendency to lose yourself in the emotions and energies of others.

When I finish my work, whether mediumistically or intuitively, I like to wash my hands and imagine that the water is washing away any energy I've dealt with that isn't mine. Even though the water is only touching my hands, I still imagine that energy being washed away from my entire body and energetic field. Another practice I use is turning on my ceiling fan and standing underneath it, letting the breeze sweep away the unwanted energy. Just like with my grounding practice, I do more if I feel the need. I might take a shower, do a workout, sing, get bodywork done, or see an energy worker.

I gave a reading for a mother who had lost her three-year-old son to drowning just six months prior. Thank goodness I was able to hold a space for her and to be clear with myself about what was the energy of the spirit and of her. I was able to give a reading that held plenty of space for her own emotions. When the reading was over, though, I needed more grounding and more clearing of my own energy. My daughter was the same age as the boy who had drowned, and in order to release the energy I'd worked with, I cried it out. I washed my hands and sat under the fan. I went for a walk. I needed it all. Sometimes readings are heavy or overwhelming for us and we need to give ourselves extra to take good care.

Energy protection exercise:

As you sit to connect with Spirit, once you are grounded, imagine a large bubble about five feet out from your body surrounding you. Strongly intend and know that this bubble will not only protect your energy from unwanted energy, but that it will bring clarity to you about moments when you're taking on energy that isn't yours so that you can become more confident about your own energetic boundaries and awareness. Sit for a minute or two and feel the confidence that comes from putting this energetic protection in place.

Creating Boundaries with Spirit

When you're just starting out as a medium, you want to sense the Spirit World all the time! It's miraculous and exciting, and you're trying to figure out how it all works. I get it, and I've been there. But if you were a doctor, you wouldn't be ready to diagnose and treat people at the grocery store, when you go out to dinner, or when you're at a social event. In fact, that'd be a major invasion of other people's privacy. The same is true for mediumship. It's not our place to dive into people's personal information by testing out whose passed loved ones we can sense at any given moment without their consent. Your abilities aren't going anywhere. They will develop efficiently whether you do a reading or two and development practices each week or readings nonstop. In fact, your progress will likely be *more* efficient if you're giving yourself down time and not constantly walking around with your spirit antennae on. I'll go as far as to say that there isn't much that's more important than establishing boundaries with Spirit in a way that conserves your energy and makes the practice of mediumship sustainable for you. If you don't, I promise you that you'll experience the wide range of symptoms that come from energetic exhaustion and burnout.

Of course, every medium is different. Some people have vast amounts of energy for group readings on large stages. Some can only do a small number of private readings per week. Some notice the differences in the energetic toll it takes to do a private reading versus a group reading. It also depends on what season of life you're in and the energetic and emotional capacity that is available to you. You won't figure this out overnight because it takes time to understand who you are as a medium and what is sustainable for you. As you learn about your mediumship, you'll find out which boundaries are most important for you. Start where you are, and be open to knowing that you will change as a medium over time. That means that your boundaries might need to shift during different seasons of life.

The thing to understand is that now is always the best time to establish your boundaries so that you can enjoy this work and do it long term if that is your desire. You teach people how to treat you, and the same is true for Spirit. Start by getting clear on what you're available for and what you're *not* available for in your relationship with Spirit. Boundaries work, but not according to what you *say* you are available for. They work according to what you *believe* and *know* you are available for.

Spiritual Boundary Exercise Part I:

Below is a quick example of a few things that I am available for, and that I am not available for, in my relationship with Spirit.

What I'm available for:

- Speaking with Spirit when I'm working professionally as a medium in any capacity or if there is an emergency
- One spirit at a time speaking to me during a reading even if others are present
- Spirits that are looking to communicate with loved ones for the purpose of peace, healing, and spiritual or human progress of any kind
- Spontaneous signs from Spirit that help to guide me on my life path

What I'm not available for:

- Spirit coming to me at any other time than when I'm teaching, reading professionally, or in an emergency
- More than one spirit speaking at once during a reading
- Any spirit or entities that are here for any other reason but healing and leaving my sitters and myself better than when they found us
- Spiritual impressions that are so intense that they bring me discomfort of any kind

Now it's your turn to identify what you're available for and not available for in your relationship with Spirit. Take some time to really think about what will make your mediumship practice sustainable and joyful for the long term.

What I'm available for:	What I'm not available for:

Spiritual Boundary Exercise Part II:

Once you've spent the time thinking through what boundaries with Spirit will bring you joy and sustainability for the long term in your work as a spiritual practitioner, it may be as simple as intending that Spirit has heard those boundaries. You can also sit down and communicate in your mind or out loud what those boundaries are. If you'd like to do that, it might sound something like this, "Hello Spirit, in order to love my work as a spiritual practitioner, here are the healthy boundaries that I'd like to put in place in our relationship." You can continue by reading your lists and strongly intending them.

Spiritual Boundary Exercise Part III:

There may be times that we feel our boundaries need to be reiterated. Sometimes this happens for me when I can tell multiple spirits are present that are excited about communicating and therefore not observing my one-at-a-time guideline.

If you feel like your boundaries aren't being observed, you can:

1. Acknowledge the spirit.
2. Say "No, not right now."
3. Tell them when (if there is a time).

In general, this sounds like, "I sense your presence, but I'd like you to know I'm not available right now. You can come back when I'm x, y, z." For me, it's "when I'm working professionally."

For the example of spirits not coming one at a time, it might sound like, "I sense that there is more than one spirit present, but I'd like the main communicator *only* to step forward. This is a reminder that I only work with one spirit at a time. For additional spirits, I'll get to as many of you as I can in the time that I have, but for now please step back."

Think of a boundary of yours that might need to be reiterated. Write a sentence below that will help you restate it to Spirit.

What If Boundaries "Don't Work?"

I've heard from mediums who feel that boundaries don't work for them. If you feel that you've tried all of this and it doesn't work, consider that you may have a blind spot in terms of where you say you have a boundary yet your beliefs and actions don't keep that boundary intact. This is not to blame or shame anyone. Certainly there are many humans who have been abused or had their boundaries violated, and these can be dangerous situations. In your relationship with Spirit, take time to be introspective about your own belief systems that may conflict with the boundaries that you desire. There's so much in our subconscious mind that can keep us a little stuck. When this happens for me, I use therapy or energy work.

Expand Your Awareness Through the Living of Daily Life

There are many powerful exercises that I've outlined in this book so far and that are still to come, but I can't overstate how effective being present in life is for mediumship development. Remember that Spirit wants us to be present here on earth. We came here to have a human experience; therefore, immersing ourselves in our life experiences is what can bring us the most growth and soul evolution. It seems like some people think that we must be focused solely or very heavily on the spiritual aspect of ourselves in order to be a great spiritual practitioner. I've found that the more present we are in our lives, the more we have the potential to grow and learn as humans and as mediums.

One of the best things you can do as a medium to expand your spiritual toolbox is to pay attention to the moment by focusing your mind on your senses. When my clients want to develop their clairvoyance, I tell them to pay close attention to the detail they are seeing in their everyday life. That might be the faces of people, the beauty of nature, and anything else their eyes can show them. If they want to improve their clairaudience, I tell them to pay close attention to the detail of the sounds that they hear each day. It might be the hum of the dishwasher, the sound of a loved one's voice, the instruments that make up their favorite song, or anything else that their ears can hear. The same is true for clairsentience. They can pay close attention to details that have to do with feeling. This might be a sensation in the body, an emotion they are feeling, or the textures we feel with physical touch. The same goes for tastes and smells. The details of the life we live every day are all pieces of information that make up our environment, our experiences, and our memories. The more we take them in, the more effective they are as a part of our spiritual toolbox that Spirit can use to communicate with us.

Never Make Assumptions

While our own frame of reference is the very thing that Spirit uses while we work mediumistically, that frame of reference can also be something that limits us. Our frame of reference is made up of our memories, knowledge, experiences, etc., and often those things make up our belief systems. While you're giving a reading, you may think that you understand the behind-the-scenes of the evidence and message that you're bringing through, and a lot of the time, you might be right. Remember, though, that as a medium, you're telling a story that you have no context for in the way that the sitter does. Spirit will often give us evidence and messages that we don't always understand but that our sitter does. As soon as we leap to assumptions about a piece of evidence here or there, it can lead us to *think* we're telling a certain kind of story, only to find out afterward from our sitter that while our evidence was spot on, the situation we were communicating about was not what we thought. The danger in this is that it's one way you can get off track and let your thinking mind become active during a reading without playing your role of simply channeling. A lot of times assumptions lead us to a more limited, one-dimensional representation of both spirits and humans.

Recall the story I told about giving a reading for a mother and her daughter and how differently the passed husband came through for one daughter versus the other. Was there anything technically wrong with my two readings where this father represented himself so differently? No, but I can tell you that if I were to give either of those readings now, it's likely I'd be less inclined to see this father as one-dimensionally as I did back when I was just beginning my mediumship journey.

Mediumship, and life, have taught me how multi-dimensional we are as humans. While I'd understood the role the father had played to some degree in that initial reading, it's more likely now that I'd understand more about his struggles and how other people in his life experienced that side of him even during my first encounter with his spirit. Because of the evidence that came through in the first reading, even though it wasn't apparent to my sitters, I had made the assumption that this father was *always* a present father and never would have suffered from addiction. It's so easy for us to bring through a few pieces of evidence and then for our brains to jump in and decide we know the kind of person this spirit was and the story that's being told. I see it all the time with my students when they bring through evidence that means something to them and then their brain orients in that direction, and they start getting nos or asking questions of their sitter that take them astray. No matter the evidence that comes through, take it at face value until the meaning behind it is communicated to you by the spirit. So many things change throughout a lifetime. Even in a short lifetime, people change and grow and have experiences that bring out the many different sides of them. Never make assumptions. Communicate the evidence as cleanly as you can.

Be Aware of Your Sitter

Your attention should, of course, be mainly focused on the spirit that you are connecting with during a reading, but it's also important that you have awareness of your sitter. As mediums, we should be pretty adept at getting a read on our sitter as soon as they sit down with us. So many of us are empaths and deeply aware of the energy of another person. We often get a feeling for them quickly in terms of their personality, but we can also get better at noticing if they are someone who is deeply grieving, feeling nervous, closed off emotionally, open emotionally, excited, etc. Based on what we notice and how their energy presents itself throughout the reading, it's important that we establish trust with them and that we have a connection with them throughout the reading.

Why is this so important? While we're merely messengers channeling communication straight from Spirit, the way in which we bring those accurate messages across and how we put things matters.

I had an experience getting a reading with an exceptional medium. She was amazingly accurate with lots of detailed evidence, but she laughed often when she brought through information. The evidence might not have seemed super heavy to her, but hearing from this person was extremely emotional for me, and she didn't seem to notice or pick up on it. I felt like I was going to start sobbing the entire time, but I never did because the way in which she presented the information didn't match up sensitivity-wise with where I was. In short, I didn't feel comfortable or safe enough to cry even though I really wanted to. This prevented me from having the healing experience that I'd really hoped for. This comes down to a lack of my awareness as the sitter. It's so common that people come to us in a very emotionally vulnerable state, and we need to be aware of this. When we get heavy, personal, or sensitive information that comes through, we need to know how to use finesse and to compassionately communicate the message in a way that is most effective and allows the sitter to take it in.

There are other times during a reading where perhaps the sitter or the audience—if you're reading in a group—needs a bit of levity after some heavily emotional messages. There might be a moment where a window for humor presents itself, and it's important to take it, but use humor in a way that is just right for the moment and not insensitive. This takes great skill in terms of being aware of your sitter and your audience. Ultimately, it's about developing your emotional intelligence. Here are a few ways to do just that:

1) Increase your awareness of self.

This might require the help of a therapist or energy worker, or just the practice of being introspective so that you are aware of your emotions and responses to life and others. It's also important to have some level of awareness about how you come across to other people when presenting evidence.

2) Practice communicating clearly with others.

Be open, straightforward, and transparent with others. Be a straight shooter.

3) Practice empathy.

If I may say so, many humans are shit at showing empathy. Empathy is about truly listening to the feelings of others and then acknowledging them. Unfortunately, most people respond to a person saying, "I'm really sad about a, b, c" by saying, "Well, it could be worse." This is not empathy because there is no understanding and acknowledgement of the person's emotional state.

4) Practice present listening.

This is another one that many humans aren't the best at. Our minds get so busy that truly being present with someone and listening without an agenda can be difficult. Practice simply listening to others and truly hearing them without an agenda and without interrupting.

5) Maintain a growth mindset.

If you're so set in your ways that you get easily put off when you speak to people who say things you don't always agree with, it's difficult to see them honestly because so much of your own bias gets in the way. Stay open and curious with others about why they say and do certain things and who they really are.

6) Welcome and take in feedback.

You may not agree with everyone's opinion, but staying open to feedback and giving consideration to it is an important aspect of emotional intelligence because it signals that you don't feel you're unavailable for growth and improvement.

Three Steps for Increased Accuracy and Added Depth in Your Readings

The great news about mediumship is that as you practice and evolve your skills, you will start to hear more yeses over time and your awareness will expand. This often brings more depth to your readings.

What do I mean by more depth? Recall the story about the father who played very different roles for his two daughters. Being able to be aware of these different aspects of him as a father in a single reading is an example of bringing more depth into my readings. I'm more able to do this now that I've been strengthening my skills over time than I was initially able to when I began my mediumship journey. Having more depth in your readings means not just being accurate in your evidence, but fleshing out your evidence so that the spirit you are channeling is more accurately represented as the multi-dimensional person that they were when they were living.

I host trainings that I call "reading assessment workshops." In them, I observe mediums while they give a fifteen-minute reading. If needed, I coach them in the moment and give feedback after the reading. A student was bringing through a passed mother for a daughter. The reading was accurate. The mother had fiercely loved her daughter, was protective, and believed in her always. It was a nice reading. When it was over, I complemented the medium for a job well done. Then I brought up the idea of bringing more depth to the reading. The reason the mother had wanted to state these feelings for her daughter was because she had been hard on her as a child. The parents had been divorced, and the father was absent. It was a time of struggle, and often the daughter was viewed as too sensitive and her feelings and struggles were overlooked. I stated this and confirmed it with the sitter. The medium was surprised that she hadn't been aware of this. I assured her she'd done a great job and that this element of depth was coming for her and would continue to show up more and more. It is something that comes in time for more mediums—and not always right from the start.

I'm sure you're wondering what you can practice to conduct more accurate readings and to bring that element of depth in as soon as possible, right? I've got three best practices to share with you that will help you with both accuracy and depth!

1) Avoid jumping to interpret meaning too quickly.

We've touched upon this idea in the Communication and Clairs section while discussing "leaning into the spiritual impression" in order to allow the impression to unfold. Jumping to interpret too quickly might look like seeing a pair of overalls clairvoyantly in your mind's eye and then immediately interpreting this image literally by deciding that your spirit wore overalls. I did this during one of my very first readings. I got a "no" from my sitter: "No, I don't remember him wearing overalls a lot, but maybe he did?" Jumping to interpret happens when we receive a spiritual impression, and without continuing to use our clair senses to sense meaning, we allow our brains to become active and make the interpretation instead. It's important to also note that jumping to interpret too quickly is different from making assumptions during a reading. While both of them have to do with your active mind making meaning of spiritual impressions, I think of "jumping to interpret" as being focused more on a single piece of evidence at a time and "assumptions" as your active mind's overall view of the entire body of evidence that you bring through during a reading. While I've framed this concept in previous sections, it's one of those things that you can't hear too many times.

Let's go back to the overalls example. You see the pair of overalls, and without sensing additional meaning behind them, you rush to the active mind's decision that this means your spirit wore overalls. You hear the "no." You've jumped to interpret too quickly. Now you see the overalls again. For a moment, you still don't *sense* meaning until suddenly, you start to get the clairsentient feeling that these overalls are not literal, but that they have symbolic meaning. You can feel the resonance within your body telling you the overalls are indeed a symbol. The next impression that falls into your mind is clairaudient, and you hear the words "tradesperson" and "plumber." You then communicate to your sitter, "Your uncle is showing me a pair of overalls. I get the sense that this is symbolic for his profession, which would have been a kind of tradesperson, for example, a plumber." Your sitter says, "Yes, he was a tradesperson. Not a plumber, but something similar!" By allowing a moment for more of your clairs to assist you and for a following spiritual impression to flow in, you were able to understand the more accurate meaning from the spirit. If you aren't *sensing* the meaning immediately, give it a moment instead of allowing your active brain to jump to interpret.

2) Avoid asking your sitter questions.

I tell all of my clients before their reading that a medium should never be prodding them with questions. Even if you're asking questions based on the legit impressions that you're receiving, it still makes you look like you're playing a guessing game instead of using your skills. This isn't to say that you can *never* ask your sitter questions. I might bring through three or four pieces of evidence and then ask my sitter a clarifying question as I sense the meaning and put the pieces together. More often, though, I make statements about what I'm sensing, and after bringing through four to five pieces of evidence or more, I will say, "Does this make sense to you?" or "Does this resonate?" or "Do you understand this?" This is a much cleaner way of working than asking lots of direct and specific questions. Just as importantly, when a medium receives a spiritual impression and jumps straight to asking their sitter a direct question, they are making a mistake that leads to a similar outcome as jumping to interpretation. Both choices lead a medium to rob themselves of using their senses to understand the meaning behind the impression.

When we jump to questioning our sitter instead of allowing our clairs to come and assist us or the next impression to follow, I call this dumping the medium's work on the sitter. It's not their job to speak to the spirit and derive the meaning of the impression. It's yours, as the medium! If you're relying on your clair senses and allowing a moment for the next impression, you won't need to ask direct questions of your sitter. Even if you aren't certain of the meaning after leaning into the impression, you can still present your evidence and ask your sitter, "Does this make sense to you?" instead of asking them a direct question about that particular impression. Allow time for your clair senses to assist you in the meaning and for spiritual impressions to follow. Present your pieces of evidence to the best of your ability, and ask your sitter if they understand the information you're bringing through.

3) Cycle through the clairs.

As you continue on in your development, you'll notice that certain clairs and certain kinds of evidence come to you more easily than others. That's normal. It's also something that you can change and expand upon. As a medium, I want to move past bringing through the same types of evidence in the same old ways. I want to continue to bring through all kinds of jaw-dropping evidence by using as many of my clairs as possible! Here is what cycling through the clairs looks like: Let's say you're giving a reading and you see those overalls clairvoyantly again. Before jumping to interpretation or asking a question of my sitter, I'd cycle through the clairs by asking, "Now what can I smell?" I start to smell something metallic. I then ask myself, "What can I feel?" I feel a little buzz in my fingers that also gives me the image of a small spark. I ask myself what I can taste. I strangely taste metal. Finally, I ask myself, "What do I know?" Instantly, the idea of an electrician drops into my mind. I share with my sitter that I see overalls, which indicate to me that this spirit was a tradesperson with a skilled craft when they were alive, and that I get the feeling they were an electrician. My sitter smiles and gives me a "yes!"

Take a moment after receiving a spiritual impression to cycle through the clairs and invite your different senses in if they aren't already working in conjunction upon the meaning of that impression. When I give my students this exercise in my development circle classes, the first thing they say is, "I hardly ever use that clair, but I did this time, and I got way more information from that single spiritual impression than I usually do!"

Not only do these three hacks help you to be more accurate with your evidence and message during a reading, but they create better, more professional habits and practices. Those habits and practices lead you to unfold more depth in your readings and, therefore, to have a more healing effect on your sitters.

When You're Ready to Go Pro

The last thing you'll ever hear me say is a specific amount of time it takes to develop your mediumship or to become a professional medium. Putting a measurement of time on mediumship development is a big no-no for me because everyone is so very different and we progress at different speeds.

Without a doubt, developing your mediumship in the direction of your full potential is a never-ending journey that takes commitment and work. In terms of when you're ready to start working professionally, it really comes down to your ability to consistently give quality readings. Below is the list of the expectations that I have if I'm going to be paying for a mediumistic reading. These are the same expectations I set for myself.

1) You can consistently identify contacts with accuracy.

This means that you can identify who is coming through and the spirit's relationship to the sitter in a reasonable amount of time. I usually get a clear sense of who a spirit is from the start of the reading, often even in the moments before the reading when no evidence has been brought through yet. Other times I lead with the personality, character, gender, and age range before getting the feeling or symbol for exactly who a spirit is in relation to the sitter. There are times when I'm unable to identify the *exact* relationship to the sitter, but the evidence and description of them is accurate, and the sitter knows who they are. For example, I might have identified a mother figure for my sitter without knowing exactly what role she played. My sitter understands who this spirit is, though, which is most important, and at the conclusion of the reading, she shares that this spirit was her mother-in-law.

2) You can consistently bring through specific, evidential information that lets your sitter know that their loved one is truly present.

Evidential mediumship is about bringing through quality evidence that can be validated by your sitter. Examples are the spirit's gender, age range, relationship to the sitter, their side of the family, details about how they passed, any pets they had, their personality and character, interactions they had with the sitter, shared memories, objects or keepsakes, their name, etc. This evidence plays a hugely significant role in providing proof of life after the death of the body and also builds trust between you and your sitter, helping them to understand and accept that their loved one in spirit is truly present and speaking to them through you.

3) You can consistently bring through a meaningful message from spirits to sitters.

Spirit doesn't show up just to give you evidential information about who they were while they were here on earth. They show up because they want to make a connection with a loved one and because they have something to say that will provide healing, peace, encouragement, etc. It *might* be a simple message such as "I love you" or "I'm at peace and no longer in pain." It could be about something going on in the sitter's life. Often the message may have elements of gratitude, forgiveness, apologies, etc. Most of the time, messages contain aspects of all these things. I've never had a reading where there wasn't more to say than just "I love you."

4) You are able to maintain a high enough vibration to speak to Spirit for at least sixty minutes at a time.

Mediumistic readings require us to work with energy and to use energy—lots of it! Every medium has a different capacity for giving readings, and some mediums read far more frequently than others. Different mediums also run their readings for different lengths of time. Usually a mediumistic reading will run for anywhere from thirty to sixty minutes. When you're ready to go pro, even if you're only giving a reading or two a week, you have to know that you can maintain a high vibration and connect to Spirit for a long enough period of time that will allow you to fulfill the promise of delivering a quality reading for a sitter.

5) You understand mediumship ethics and professionalism.

Definitely revisit the section in this book about mediumship ethics if you feel fuzzy on this topic.

Please also visit my YouTube channel @mediumshipwithmel using the QR code below to watch this video, *"What You Should Know About Mediumship Ethics."*

6) The pressure of receiving payment for your services doesn't shut down your ability to channel spirit.

Part of becoming a professional medium is accepting payment for your services. For a lot of mediums, this is a big deal. As a former business consultant and online marketing strategist, I know how difficult it can be to have the courage and confidence to charge without crumbling under the pressure. I could write an entire book about why being willing to accept payment for the hard and incredibly important work that we do as mediums is an absolute must.

So many mediums struggle with feeling guilty about charging for one reason or another. Many times this comes down to how some mediums think of their own self worth, but I find that it also has to do with belief systems that we, as an industry, have created around how the work of a medium is different from other "normal" jobs. Perhaps you view this work as more sacred than other occupations or as being emotionally high stakes for the sitter—or you might suffer from the pressure of needing to get it perfect once you decide to charge for your services.

If any of this resonates with you and contributes to feelings of guilt or discomfort about charging your clients, consider that many professionals provide services that are considered sacred in some way *and* get paid, like priests, therapists and teachers. Other practitioners and professionals also feel the great responsibility of their work, like surgeons, EMTs, ambulance drivers, and firefighters. There are plenty of people who work jobs where accuracy matters but perfection is not the expectation. Consider economists, weather people, doctors, and project managers.

When you feel that you're nearing the time when you're ready to start working professionally and receiving payment, think about ways that you can ease into that pressure of receiving without the guilt! Perhaps to start you give shorter readings at a lower cost. Maybe you do donation-based readings for a fixed amount of time while you adjust to getting paid some amount of money and build up your confidence. Go at a pace that feels comfortable to you. It's never a good idea to charge a lot more than you're comfortable with just because someone tells you you should. That's a quick way to kill your momentum and put more pressure than is necessary on yourself as you work.

Remember, though, that the work you do has the potential to be life-changing and is some of the most rewarding and meaningful work out there. You give so much of yourself to bring others comfort, peace, relief, and healing. You'll be able to work joyfully and more sustainably if you allow yourself the proper energetic exchange for what you do, and there is no need to feel guilty or apologize for that.

Conclusion

I'm beyond honored that you spent your time with this book. I know there are countless mentors, instructional videos, and books that you could have chosen to put your minutes and hours into instead. As you move forward on your journey as a medium, I would love nothing more than for this book to be something that you come back to time and time again. May you highlight the shit out of it, bookmark pages, and go far beyond simply using it as a doormat or coaster.

Take what resonates with you, and leave what doesn't. There are so many ways to practice mediumship, and my wish is that you feel rich with the golden nuggets that you've discovered within this book, but that you discover many of your own as you move forward on your path, too.

While I am a strong believer in the five Cs, and I feel that each of them can help take you to the next level, please do take the Command of Craft C to heart. Get specific about the aspects of your practice that you sense and believe hold the greatest opportunities for your growth. Be relentless in your development, and shoot for the stars. You'll surprise yourself in the best way.

Most definitely, work to develop your own sense of resonance and dissonance. It's not to say that feedback from trusted sources isn't valuable and very much needed at times, but let these tools be your guide rather than making a habit of seeking validation outside of yourself.

Of course, I can't let you close this book without reminding once more to never accept the limitations that any other person might try to put on you. You are unique and different from any other medium currently on the planet—and from any mediums who came before you. Enjoy and trust your developmental path, and remain curious about who *you* are as a medium and what *your* style looks like.

Just know it's about you a little bit, but mostly it's so much bigger than any one individual person. I beg you, take the time to truly ask yourself how you can use these skills for good. What is the difference you're hungry to make, for the better, in this world? And when you answer that question, promise me you'll think big.

You're not doing this alone. The invitation always stands to join me, in my community, on this mediumship journey of yours. You're always welcome to partake in my courses or development circles, or to simply binge my free online content. Ultimately, keep me in your back pocket so we can nerd out together about Spirit.

Acknowledgments

Making the time to write this book was most definitely a choice, but as with all things, it didn't happen without the support of remarkable people. To Sara, you are the person who sees people as authors before they see it themselves. From the moment we met, I knew I had at least three books in me. To Aubyn, my editor, for giving it to me straight and truly seeing me from the very beginning. To my daughters, you inspire me more than you'll ever know to be all that I can be for myself, for you, and for all. To my mom and dear friend, Christine, I offer my endless gratitude. You showed me what a woman who wastes no time wondering if she's capable can do. To Rob, the love of my life and soulmate, you are the best decision I've made. Your unconditional love and belief in me is one of the greatest gifts a partner can give.

About the Author

Melissa Pharr is a professional spiritual medium, mom, wife, and businesswoman. She didn't pop out seeing dead people as a kid (at least not that she can remember) and never imagined running a business as a spiritual practitioner. She now sells out mediumship development circles, mediumship readings, and courses of all kinds, bringing peace and closure to those who sit with her and a down-to-earth and straightforward approach to mediumship for aspiring mediums. Mel has studied residentially at the Arthur Findlay College in Essex, UK, and continues her studies via tutors, mediumship development circles, and trainings with the Arthur Findlay College and the Journey Within Spiritualist Church.